C000212427

Who Killed Simon Dale?

Who Killed Simon Dale?
& other murder mysteries

by
Kate Clarke

Logaston Press
1993

LOGASTON PRESS
Little Logaston Woonton Almeley
Herefordshire HR3 6QH

First published by Logaston Press 1993
Copyright © Kate Clarke 1993

All rights reserved. No part of this publication
may be reproduced, stored in a retrieval system,
or transmitted, in any form or by any means,
electronic, mechanical, photocopying, recording
or otherwise, without the prior permission,
in writing, of the publisher

ISBN 1 873827 03 2

Phototset in Times 11/13 pt by Logaston Press
and printed in Great Britain
by Ebenezer Baylis & Son, Worcester

Contents

Acknowledgements

I should like to thank the following persons for their help and encouragement during the writing of this book:

Mr Dean Anderson, Mr Jamie Awson, Mr Terry Babington, Mrs Diana Blunt, Mr F Bond, Mr J Bourne, Mrs Bernice Brown, Mr Dewi Davies, Mr Bob Dew, Mr Richard Hammonds, Mr Douglas Maclean, Mr Bernard Taylor, Mr Sid Wilding and Mrs Fiona Willets.

Further thanks should go to Mrs Carol Robinson and Mr Robin Hill at Hereford Reference Library, Mr Price at Brecon Reference Library, Mrs Betty Jones at Hay Public Library and journalist Mr Nigel Heins, author of the *Flashback* series in *The Hereford Times*.

I should also like to acknowledge the friendship and support of Martin and Noelle Beales and Syd and Anne Gedge, and to thank Sasha Clarke for her invaluable searches at the British Newspaper Library at Colindale, London; and Paul Latcham for permission to reproduce the illustration of Weobley on page 69 from *Nooks and Corners of Herefordshire*.

Especial thanks must also go to Jennifer Green, for her generosity in allowing me to use her book, the only major study of the Mary Morgan case *The Morning of Her Day*, first published by Divine Books in 1987. Re-issued by Darf Publishers in 1990 and soon to become the subject of a film.

Foreword

Whilst there are many thousands of murders committed around the world each year the motives seem surprisingly few and have changed little over the centuries. Most people find murder interesting; is it, perhaps, because the underlying passions that result in murder are common to us all, though in the case of murderers they are magnified, distorted and out of control? And is it our innate fear of violent death that enables us to so readily identify with the victim? Here lies the dual fascination with murder. And that astute criminologist, William Roughead, was right when he said that murder has 'a magic of its own, its peculiar alchemy. Touched by that crimson wand, things base and sordid, things ugly and of ill report, are transformed into matters wondrous, weird and tragical. Dull streets become fraught with mystery, commonplace dwellings assume sinister aspects, everyone concerned, howsoever plain and ordinary, is invested with a new value and importance as the red light falls upon each.'

This book covers fourteen cases of murder scattered either side of the border of England and Wales, stories that tell of the devastating effect of obsessive love, concealed hatred, of lust, greed and revenge and clearly illustrate the part played by the acute poverty and ignorance of times past and the violence unleashed by drink.

As, during much of the period covered, convicted murderers were killed by hanging it may be worth recording something of its history. Whilst some of the cases recorded here would still be regarded as open and shut convictions, in one the person found quilty would almost certainly not have been if the trial had taken place in the 1990's.

The method of judicial hanging is thought to have originated in Persia, spreading to continental Europe with the Huns, and to England with the Anglo-Saxons. Originally, those convicted were simply strung from the branch of a tree, later refined to a gallows. But the course of death was still the same—slow strangulation.

In the United Kingdom it was only in 1760 that a gallows was designed to cause fracture of the neck and a quick death by means of a drop, a trap-door through which the victim fell to be brought up sharply by the pull of the rope.

However, at the time of the first case recorded in this book, in the latter 1700's, not just the gallows but the gibbet would have been a familiar sight. The murderer's corpse was chained to the gibbet in full view of the neighbours until it rotted away. This disgusting practice was greatly frowned upon, not necessarily on humanitarian grounds but because of the adverse effect on the value of property in the vicinity of the gibbet! An article in *The Hereford Times*, dated 4 August, 1832, draws attention to the problem:

'The clause in the Anatomy Bill ordering the bodies of murderers to be hung in chains is one of so offensive a nature that it cannot long be put in force... Wherever a gibbet is erected, (except upon some wild unfrequented heath, and then it has no effect), the value of household property is reduced one half. Indeed, not one in ten would live in a place where such a spectacle could be seen from the windows, or where there might be a risk of coming in view of it on excursions in the neighbourhood.

'And supposing the law to be put in force for a number of years, there would hardly be a district in England without a gibbeted murderer, which, instead of acting as a check on the living, tends rather to harden the wicked and to blunt the feelings of persons of every description. It is wellknown that frequent executions diminish the terror of death and it is no less true that the more frequent such exhibitions as those alluded to should become throughout the country, their effect on the inhabitants would be proportionately lessened.

'The people of this country, with a natural abhorrence of such exhibitions, have not unfrequently removed them of their own

accord; and the clause in the Bill, making such conduct a transportable offence, will not be sufficient to deter them from abating what they consider not only a nuisance but a needless deterioration of property.'

It was also customary for the convicted prisoner to be allowed to address the hostile crowd that almost invariably gathered round the gallows. Many couldn't face the ordeal, or perhaps were too inarticulate to manage more than a few words. Others like Colonel John Turner, sentenced in 1664 to hang for robbery, chose to exercise his right. Hoping to delay his execution long enough for a reprieve to be granted, he embarked on a monumental speech relating his whole life history, including his experience as a Cavalier in the recent Civil War. But this ingenious attempt to cheat death failed and he was duly hanged.

For murder was not the only crime to carry the death sentence. In the early 1800's there were more than two hundred capital offences on the statute book. Men, women and even children as young as eight or nine were hanged for stealing items of little value and public hangings and floggings were commonplace well into the nineteenth century.

However, in 1830, due to the efforts of enlightened prison reformers like Samuel Romilly, the number of offences carrying the death sentence was substantially reduced.

Charles Dickens, amongst others, voiced his concerns at the sickening behaviour of the crowds attending public hangings, stating that a public execution was 'a savage horror far behind the time.' They were abolished in 1868.

With hanging then confined within the relative privacy of the prison walls it was no longer necessary to pander to the population's thirst for gory spectacle—Calcraft, public executioner from 1829 to 1874 when he retired aged 73, was notoriously clumsy, often having to pull on the prisoner's legs and rarely administering a clean death—and attention focused on perfecting a technique that was as humane as possible. The Yorkshire born hangman, James Berry, a cobbler by trade, who held office from 1884 to 1892, devised a system of drops based on the weight of the prisoner. Yet Berry, like all men who kill 'out of duty', was blithely convinced that his calling justified his annihilation of more than two hundred people, and felt no pity whatsoever for those condemned for killing illegally.

It is satisfying, therefore, to record that one person did manage to escape Berry's noose. Only a year before he executed Hill and Williams (a case detailed in this book), right at the start of his grotesque career, Berry tried to hang a man called John Lee—and failed. In 1884, Lee, a footman, was convicted of murdering his elderly employer and sentenced to death. James Berry arrived at Exeter prison, made all the prior arrangements but found, after placing Lee on the scaffold and pulling the lever, that nothing happened. Determined to perform his duty he furiously waggled the lever several times and even stamped on the trap doors. Still they stayed closed. The wretched prisoner was taken away and the equipment tested—a dummy run with a substitute weight worked perfectly. Yet, when Berry tried to hang Lee a second time, the doors remained firmly shut.

Incredibly, Lee was brought to the scaffold for the third time but again the apparatus failed to work. At this point the execution was cancelled and Lee, who said he had dreamed that he would not hang, was granted a reprieve. Ascribing this extraordinary episode to divine intervention he still served twenty-two years in prison. He was released in 1907 and died, aged sixty-eight, in 1933. Berry was loathe to imagine for one moment that God could side with a convicted killer, and always maintained that warped wood, not divine mercy, was to blame.

But the most remembered hangman, if only because he was one of the most recent, was Albert Pierrepoint. Both his father, Henry, and his uncle, Thomas, had been executioners before him. Albert commenced his work in 1931, retiring in 1956, during which time he hanged more than five hundred men and women—including a number of war criminals and the last woman to hang in Great Britain, Ruth Ellis. He applied his craft with meticulous care to ensure that death was always by instantaneous dislocation, not strangulation.

Finally, the death penalty for murder was ended with the passing of The Abolition of the Death Penalty Act in December, 1964, though repeated calls are made in Parliament for its return. It is worth reflecting, therefore, on the words Albert Pierrepoint wrote in the forward to his his autobiography, published in 1974:

'It is a fact which is no source of pride to me at all—it is simple history—that I have carried out the execution of more judicial sentences of death, (outside the field of politics), than any executioner in any British record or archive. That fact is the measure of my experience. The fruit of my experience has this bitter after-taste; that I do not now believe that any one of the hundreds of executions I carried out has in any way acted as a deterrent against future murder. Capital punishment, in my view, achieved nothing except revenge.'

Kate Clarke
May 1993

I

Arsenic in the soup

The village of Clodock, on the south west border of Hereford-shire, lies in the shadow of the Black Mountains, and has been the scene of many a bloody skirmish between the Marcher barons and the Welsh rebels during the fourteenth and fifteenth centuries. It was here, in the fifth century, that Prince Clydawg, son of the king of Ewyas, met with a violent death. According to the *Liber Landavensis*, 'a certain young woman, daughter of a wealthy man, was in love with him and said to those who sought her that she would marry no one but the illustrious Clydawg.' Unfortu-nately, the chaste and godly Clydawg, described as 'innocent as a lamb', did not return her affection. Far from harbouring any reciprocal lust for the young lady, he chose instead to meditate 'with great devotion on sacred subjects'. Despite his indifference, he was killed by a jealous rival whilst hunting on the banks of the River Monnow. On the day of the burial his body was placed on a cart drawn by oxen. However, as the sorrowful procession reached the ford of the river the two beasts flatly refused to cross it; despite the use of chains and ropes and repeated goading they would go no further. Reading this as a sign of divine intervention the young prince was buried there and then by the banks of the river; over the years he was remembered as a martyr, St Clydawg, and the tomb became a place of pilgrimage.

The Norman church that now stands near the site was once a 'place of refuge' during the border troubles. It also houses a number of ancient memorial stones, some thought to date from between AD 750 and 850. There is a fine 17th century triple pulpit, a musician's gallery, and box pews. There are also some early wall paintings, and at one time, a pair of especially designed tongs to seize any dogs that dared to wander into the church during services and distract the attention of the worshippers from the uplifting oratory of the preacher.

The story of William Jones and Suzannah Rugg, however, unlike that of St Clydawg, is one of earthly lust and a far from saintly end. The year was 1790, and the course of the drama began in the village of Clodock and ended on the gibbet at Longtown. At the centre of the tragedy lay that perennial domestic time-bomb—the love triangle, one man and two women, which in this case resulted in the death of all three protagonists.

Twenty-seven year old William Jones, a married man with two young children, became infatuated with an eighteen year old girl called Suzannah Rugg, from Monmouth. So besotted, in fact, that he eventually decided to leave his wife, Ann, and set up house with the teenager. Not long afterwards Jones seems to have had a change of heart and there followed a reconciliation with his wife. He returned to the family home in Clodock, giving every appearance of reform, treating Ann with unprecedented kindness and concern. His intentions, though, were duplicity itself. Once more the recipient of his wife's trust he prepared for her a bowl of gruel—which he proceeded to lace with arsenic. The poor woman died in agony on Saturday, 27 March, 1790.

The sudden death of the young mother required, of course, some enquiry and a postmortem examination was ordered. Incredibly, one of those present to witness the grisly process was her husband, William. More remarkable still, far from being distraught as the surgeon opened up Ann's stomach to reveal a quantity of arsenic, Williams showed 'not the smallest concern or surprise'.

This wholly inappropriate behaviour was, of course, considered somewhat suspicious and led to his subsequent arrest on the charge of murdering his wife, as announced in the forerunner of *The Hereford Times*, *The Hereford Journal*. His young mistress, Suzannah, was 'also committed to the (same) gaol, charged with stealing a silver watch and six shillings and six pence from Thomas Prosser, of Clodock: and also on violent suspicion of being concerned in purchasing a quantity of arsenic in company with William Jones...'

She was subsequently charged with the murder of her rival and the pair stood trial at the Hereford Assizes in the City Hall, High Town. Though the evidence against them was purely circumstantial, in that no one had seen either of them peppering the gruel with arsenic, they had the opportunity and the motive. But the most damning evidence against them was the fact that the post-mortem revealed that Ann Jones had been poisoned with an unusual mixture of yellow and white arsenic. These events were long before there were any laws concerning the sale of noxious substances. The Pharmacy Act of 1851 restricted the sale of arsenic but the more stringent Sale of Poisons Act was not introduced until 1852; it required the purchaser of listed poisons to be introduced to retailers by a person known to them and to sign the Poison Book on completion of the sale. As an additional safeguard against arsenic being mistaken for one of the many patent medicines in white powder form or any common household powders such as bicarbonate of soda, flour or salt, the chemist was obliged to colour the arsenic; an indigo-blue dye was sometimes used but more often than not a little charcoal was added.

But in 1790 there were no such formalities and anyone could buy poison over the counter, usually for killing vermin such as cats, rats and unwanted individuals. Unfortunately for the lovers the prosecution was able to produce a local apothecary prepared to swear that he had accidentally mixed a quantity of white and yellow arsenic and had inadvertently sold it to Jones and Rugg. Had he not made this mistake and sold them arsenic of consistent colour—either white or yellow—the case against them would have been almost impossible to prove.

Jones and his young girlfriend were found guilty of murdering Ann Jones and sentenced to death. At a time when crime was rife and more than two hundred offences, such as petty theft, were capital offences, hanging was 'of a melancholy frequency'. It was also carried out in full view of raucous and blood-thirsty crowds that flocked to see the appalling spectacle as if to a place of entertainment and as though death was just another amusing sideshow. This barbarity continued until its abolition in 1868. Thomas Watkins, convicted of killing his wife in 1864, was the last man to be publicly executed at Hereford.

The site for the execution of William Jones and Suzannah Rugg was opposite the gaol in St Owen Street, now St Peter's Square. Their fellow prisoners were taken from their cells and compelled to watch. According to a contemporary report, Jones and Rugg were 'perfectly penitent and resigned'. Suzannah, it appears, with amazing composure for one so young and in such terrible circumstances, urged the onlookers to choose wisely the company they kept and so avoid a similar fate. She was described as a 'beautiful girl'.

Some superstitious women in the crowd who were suffering from warts and other skin eruptions, especially on their necks, reached to touch the dying couple's hands, hoping for relief.

A gentleman who witnessed the hanging spoke of Suzannah's youth and her 'wretched mode of life' and clearly feeling tremendous sympathy for her, added: 'though justice might make the sacrifice necessary, humanity may be permitted to shed a tear for the victim'.

Shortly before he died, Jones ensured that an income of £40 a year, (a considerable sum in 1790), from his property would go to his two children, left orphans by the tragedy.

It was said that the thought of the gibbet filled most convicted criminals with dread. Unfortunately, it was this fate that awaited the corpse of William Jones; it was lifted from the scaffold and taken to the village green at Longtown, close to Clodock, where it was to hang in chains, as a constant warning to any other would-be adulterers who might be contemplating the removal of their wives.

II

The Case of the Longtown Harriers

Remarkably, for such a small village, Clodock was to witness yet another tragic, needless death, that of William Prosser, victim of a bunch of relentless bullies. The story begins with a funeral on 12 January, 1893, a particularly cold day in a harsh winter. There had already been several heavy falls of snow; it lay thick on the ground, muffling sound and changing completely the familiar pattern of track and hedgerow.

Immediately after the burial, some of the mourners hastened to The Cornewall Arms to warm their blood and lift their spirits. In an effort to dispel the gloom of the funeral someone worked the melodeon and before long the party were singing, dancing and downing tankards of hot beer spiced with rum—known locally as 'rum hot'. In one corner, playing a tune on his wooden whistle, was a labourer, William Prosser, a weedy sort of chap who lived alone with his ferret.

By the time the revellers staggered out of the pub that night the temperature was well below freezing. Most of the drinkers made their way home, feeling their way, clumsily slipping and sliding on the icy roadway, no doubt shrieking with laughter as they tried to stay upright.

But six of them—Walter Griffiths, William Davies, Leonard Miles, John Williams, Thomas Jones and Charles Lewis—did not go straight home to their cottages; they were very drunk indeed and far from ready to retire for the night. They were full of 'rum hot' and looking for some fun but the drink turned them into predators looking for prey and like all bullies they sought their enjoyment at the expense of another's distress. They headed for a barn close by where they knew John Cross, a stonemason from Leominster, was sleeping.

The six hooligans found great sport in dragging the man into the snow and rolling him over, time and time again, until he was bruised and bitterly cold. He eventually managed to escape from the gang and ran to The Cornewall Arms where the landlady, Helen Townsend, let him sit by the fire and thaw out.

Not content with the damage they'd already done, the six drunks found another victim, a wheelwright named Edwin Chappell. Pulled from his bed and dragged over his garden wall, the bullies hauled him to the banks of the River Monnow, where he was rolled in the snow and then ducked in the water.

When they tired of tormenting Chappell they remembered seeing William Prosser in the pub that evening. He would be the perfect butt for their mindless cruelty and they knew where to find him. They were well and truly on the rampage now, charging across the bridge to the other side of the river and up a steep track to Hunthouse Cottage. They started by smashing his windows and shouting obscenities. Jumping out of bed, the trembling Prosser made for the door in a desperate attempt to run for it but the bullies gave chase, caught him, and began rolling him on the ground. The freezing snow soaked into his frail body, covered only in the trousers, shirt and waistcoat he'd managed to drag on when his ordeal began.

Then, as the drunken bullies eventually began to tire he managed to escape their clutches. He ran off towards a cottage called The Garn, some distance away, and hammered on the door; but it was the middle of the night and before anyone had time to let him in, he heard the raucous shouts of his tormentors as they bore down on him once more. His nightmare was not yet over.

The terrified man ran off again, the bullies in hot pursuit, shouting abuse and taunting him as they ran. It is not known at what point they finally tired of chasing their prey. Perhaps they, too, had begun to feel the intense cold and had started to sober up. But the tragic result of the remorseless pursuit of their victim was there for all to see the next morning; the body of William

Prosser was found hanging by his waistcoat from the pointed upright of a cottage gate. Exhausted, he'd found himself caught on the jagged post and, paralysed with fear, he had been unable to disentangle himself. And there, hanging like some pitiful sacrifice, he had frozen to death—his dead eyes turned towards the church of St Clydawg.

The blame for William Prosser's death lay squarely with the six bullies and the excess of alcohol they had consumed that evening. The regulars at The Cornewall Arms, seeing the ugly mood of the revellers, could guess who was to blame, but *The Hereford Times* reported that 'the inhabitants possess the reputation, rightly or wrongly, of being a singularly clannish class. So much so indeed that police found themselves handicapped by the reticence of those who were suspected to know a great deal more than they feel disposed to divulge.' It was one of the bullies, young Charles Lewis, only seventeen and a lad of good character, who admitted his part in the outrage and his information led to the arrest of the others.

The trial of the six men, on a charge of 'feloniously killing William Prosser', was held at the Hereford Winter Assizes in March 1893. Whilst the prosecution blamed the 'rum hot' for the men's 'mischievous and wicked' behaviour, the defence counsel tried to dismiss it as merely an excess of high spirits, a 'lark' that went badly wrong. For it seems that the bullies were not the only drunkards in the village, an observer at their trial stated 'Total abstinence from intoxicating liquors is not one of the cardinal virtues of the parish...and a funeral is as good as a fair to the publicans.'

None of the defendants had any previous record of violent or disruptive behaviour and their neighbours rallied to their defence; indeed, witnesses came forward to testify that they were all hardworking men of good character. Mr Justice Grantham, whilst saying that 'drunkenness was no excuse for crime' and that 'cursed drink had brought so many men to their graves and many men to the scaffold', nevertheless took the men's previous good behaviour into account when sentencing. In his opinion, Walter Griffiths, described as a 'quiet and respectable' farmworker, and

William Davies, a miller and a 'very respectable man with a wife and young family', were the two ringleaders. He therefore sentenced them to twelve months imprisonment with hard labour. Leonard Miles, a 'man of excellent character' and father of three, had, the court was told, lent money to his victim on a number of occasions; he was given four months imprisonment with hard labour. So, too, was another member of the gang, John Williams, who, the court was assured, was a 'hardworking, respectable man'. Thomas Jones, described as 'a steady, respectable lad' was also sent to prison for four months.

Lastly, the judge addressed seventeen year old Lewis, who, as an orphan, 'had no one to direct or guide him on entering into life', saying: 'I think I am justified in assuming that you did not take anything like the part in the affair as the others did, but on the other hand, that you did your best to stop them... and made a clean breast of the matter. On the suggestion of the Crown, therefore, I am willing to deal with you in a different way from the other men. The sentence upon you will be that you be imprisoned for three days.'

William Prosser, the man with the wooden whistle and only his ferret for company, lies in his final resting place amongst the tightly-packed memorial stones beside St Clydawg's Church—once more a place of refuge—close by the gate on which he was hanged. Abutting the wall stands The Cornewall Arms, where his nightmare began that January night in 1893—and the licensee's name is Prosser.

III

The Tragic Case of Mary Morgan

Though Presteigne is more familiarly connected with Mary Morgan, her story begins at Llowes, a small hamlet near the border town of Hay. This corner of Radnorshire, close to the River Wye and the Black Mountains, has always been a sparsely populated agricultural area. Although at one time it was a self-sufficient community large enough to warrant a school, a mill, granary and forge, none of these remain. Today the schoolhouse is a private dwelling and there are only a few of the old cottages left, hidden amongst a crop of relatively modern houses. And there is no village green, pond or post office—not even a shop. There is, however, a parish church, St Meilig's, and an early drovers' venue, The Radnor Arms, unfortunately now marooned on the far side of the Hereford to Brecon road.

It was in Llowes that Mary was born in the spring of 1788 to Reece and Elizabeth Morgan. Further details of her background and early life are not known but one may assume that she was born into a relatively poor farm-worker's family and had a number of siblings. This assumption is borne out by her being put into domestic service at an early age to lighten the burden at home.

There were only a couple of great houses in the area—Llowes Court and Maesllwych,* at Glasbury. Fate would have it that a

---

* The present castellated building, Maesllwych Castle, replaced an earlier house in the mid-19th century, some years after Mary's death. It was here that the diarist, Francis Kilvert, often dined with the antecedants of the present occupants, the de Winton family.

suitable post was found for Mary in the kitchens at Maesllwych, the home of the wealthy and influential Walter Wilkins and his family. Born at Brecon in 1741, Wilkins joined the Indian Civil Service soon after completing his education and was eventually appointed Governor of Chittygong. Undoubtedly, men such as he, with interests in the East India Company, made full use of their positions of power and profiteering was widespread; so it was that, when he returned to Great Britain—still only thirty years old—he was already wealthy and well-connected.

Soon after his return Wilkins was appointed Justice of the Peace for Radnorshire and by 1774 he was made High Sheriff. He was also wealthy enough to establish the Wilkins Bank in Brecon and purchase the substantial Maesllwych estate overlooking the river at Glasbury. His good fortune was further increased by a financially prudent marriage—to Catherine, only daughter of Samuel Haywood, of Walsworth Hall, Gloucester. When his son and namesake was born Walter Wilkins seemed to have it all— power, money, prestige and now, a son and heir. But to further enhance his reputation a seat at Westminster seemed appropriate. He stood for the County seat of Presteigne and, having spent a considerable sum on wooing the voters, was successful in being elected to Westminster.

This was the social world into which Mary came into contact when she went to work for Walter Wilkins at Maesllwych as a kitchen maid earning less than £4 a year. It was a far cry from her previous life of poverty in overcrowded, insanitary conditions and as Maesllwych was only about a mile from her home she was able to walk across the fields to visit her family and friends on her occasional days off.

Not that Mary, barely fourteen, would have been allowed much time for leisure. Landed gentry like the Wilkinses would have entertained on a lavish scale and accommodated a great many house guests of the hunting, shooting and fishing brigade. Along with the rest of the domestic staff her working day would have been long and arduous. She would have been expected to rise soon after dawn to see to the fires, stoke the kitchen range and build up the heat ready for the day's baking. She would then prepare vegetables, clean and scrub the kitchen and generally do whatever Elizabeth Evelyn, the cook, required of her, often until late at night. The estate and its gardens would have provided the household with meat, game, fruit and vegetables throughout the year and one of Mary's duties would have been to slaughter, pluck, gut and prepare rabbit, fish and fowl for the pot.

Other servants, such as Mrs Simpson, the housekeeper, with her retinue of chambermaids and parlour maids, would maintain the smooth running of the household, see that the clothes, linen and draperies were laundered, mended and ironed and the furniture pristine and polished. Outside, the grooms, coachmen, and gardeners would have worked equally hard on the grounds and stables to ensure the degree of luxury that the Wilkins family and their friends accepted as their due.

Young Mary Morgan obviously proved satisfactory for by 1804 she had been promoted to the position of under-cook. Contemporary reports describe her as intelligent, extremely pretty and of good disposition. It was also remarked that she had an air of naivety or innocence about her, although she did admit to a romantic liaison with a fellow servant, of whom little is known. It was common knowledge also that the young squire of the house, Walter Wilkins, junior, by now in his early twenties, was much taken with her. It seems it was the usual story, the sons of wealthy families finding the young servant girls attractive and sometimes willing, but by no means always. It was customary for them to feel entitled to practice their sexual skills on these unfortunate working girls, for whom they had little respect, in preparation for marriage to young ladies of their own class.

It was an appalling situation for any young girl who, finding this arrangement abhorrent would, nevertheless, think twice before complaining. If she did she would probably lose her job, be sent home in disgrace, and even find herself branded a liar, a promiscuous hussy or a trouble-maker into the bargain. It must be said that whilst some girls may well have welcomed or been indifferent to these dalliances, many others must have dreaded the attentions of these privileged and often callous young men—and, if from a God-fearing family, suffered the most terrible feelings of guilt.

Either way all these young women had one thing in common—the fear of pregnancy. If it happened, months of worry and concealment followed, and if the birth was live and discovered, the outcome would be instant dismissal. It is generally accepted that many illegitimate children were conveniently smothered at birth, given away or sold and the courts heard a great many 'bastardy' and 'child-farming' cases.

It was a tragic situation, for these young mothers, barely able to support themselves and coming from families already on the breadline, could find themselves with no work, no home and the responsibility for a life other than their own.

Such was Mary Morgan's dilemma in the spring of 1804 when, at sixteen, she realised she was pregnant. According to the evidence given at her subsequent trial her fellow servants at Maesllwych had noticed that Mary, although she was working as usual on the morning of Sunday, 23 September, 1804, was clearly unwell. Until that time she had managed to conceal her condition although she had, at an earlier stage, told young Walter Wilkins that she was pregnant. According to her version of events he had offered to maintain the child after its birth provided she named him as the father. One cannot imagine why young Walter would give his name to another man's child and in doing so risk a scandal that might jeopardise his chances with Catherine Devereaux* unless he was the father; yet Mary refused to accept his offer, insisting that he was not responsible. It may be assumed therefore that the father of the child was her other lover, the fellow servant. Again, according to Mary, he, on being told that she was pregnant, had offered her a drink containing a herb which would bring about an abortion but she had refused to take it. It was therefore Mary's choice to allow the pregnancy to go full term and not terminate it. Why, when her future employment was clearly so perilous, did she insist on producing the child? Did she, perhaps, as many young women have done before her and since, hope that her lover would have a change of heart and marry her once the child was born?

* Walter Wilkins, the young squire, married Catherine Devereaux, daughter of Lord Hereford, in 1806, a year after Mary's death.

Whatever the hopes and schemes that filled young Mary's head, by one o'clock that Sunday she was in such pain she could not carry on and, taking the advice of the other servants, went up to her room to lie down. Most probably the other women in the household had by now guessed the nature of Mary's indisposition for, according to the evidence of the cook, Elizabeth Evelyn, about three o'clock in the afternoon Mrs Simpson, the house-keeper, gave her some warm wine to ease the pain in her stomach. Margaret Havard, who had replaced Mary when she was taken ill that day, testified that she had seen Mary 'about four of the clock in the afternoon being then very ill'.

Some time during the early part of the evening Mary Meredith, the under dairymaid, had returned to the house after visiting her sister. She went up to the room she shared with Mary to change out of her best clothes. When she found the door fastened she called to Mary to open it but she refused, asking to be left in peace so she could sleep.

When the cook and Margaret Havard went up again between six and seven o'clock with some tea they were allowed in and told Mary she looked 'like a woman in labour which she strongly denied.'

Mary had then begged the women not to send anyone else up and when Margaret returned about half an hour later she found that Mary had once more locked the room. She went downstairs again to fetch the cook and together they persuaded Mary to open the door. They took one look at Mary on the bed and 'accused her of having delivered herself of a child...' But she strongly denied it 'with bitter oaths for some time'. The poor girl eventually admitted that she had given birth and then showed the horrified women the dead baby 'cut open deep sunk in the feathers [of the mattress or underbed] with the child's head nearly divided from the body'. The penknife she had used was 'found by the cook bloody under the pillow of the same bed the next morning following being Monday, 24 September 1804.'

It may be that Mary, young and inexperienced, had somehow miscalculated the date of her confinement—perhaps intending to have the child on a visit home—but, finding herself going into labour in her master's house, then full of weekend guests, took the silver penknife, (which she said young Walter had given her), to cut the umbilical cord. Perhaps, in her pain and isolation she had not thought further than this—had not intended to kill the child—until, that is, once it was born, its piercing screams echoed through the attics of the great house, threatening to expose her. Was it then that she panicked and, seizing the knife once more, severed the child's tiny neck, much as she had done so often to the rabbits, ducks and hens she had killed for the table?

Walter Wilkins was informed and, as High Sheriff of Radnor, he had little choice but to alert the authorities. The County Coroner, Hector Appleby Cooksey, arrived at Maesllwych two days later and, having ascertained that the crime of infanticide had been committed, summoned a Grand Jury so that committal proceedings might be brought against Mary Morgan without delay. Meanwhile, she was arrested and taken to the gaol at Presteigne, the cost of the journey to be taken from her meagre wages.

For the next six months, Mary was incarcerated in appalling conditions, confined in a damp, rat-infested cell underneath the Shire Hall in Presteigne, the only light coming from the iron grid level with the street. Conditions in gaol in 1805 must have been grim. Those at Brecon and other prisons are well documented and there is no reason to believe that conditions at Presteigne were any different. Class I prisoners were those who were lucky enough to have family and friends who could supplement their prison rations with a little meat or even some coal to heat their cells in winter. Mary was probably in the Class 2 category, that is, entirely dependent on her daily sustenance ration of food which was one and a half pounds of bread. It is doubtful whether her family could have travelled from Llowes to Presteigne, a distance of some thirty miles, very often, if at all. It was customary for compassionate local persons to give prisoners extra food or clothing or even a little money with which to buy ale.

In *The Gentleman's Magazine* there was an article by prison campaigner, Mr Neild, about the conditions he found during a visit to Brecon County Gaol. He wrote: 'On my visit in 1803 the prisoners complained to me of being cruelly treated and half-starved. They were literally half-naked, and two women without shoes or stockings were heavily loaded with double irons... The countenances of all the prisoners bespoke neglect and oppression, and the learned Judge to whom I sent my remarks was pleaded to mention in his charge to the Grand Jury at the next assize, when the magistrates humanely interfered.' In consequence of this the gaoler was sacked and, for a while at least, there was a slight improvement in conditions.

The judge who was so concerned about the plight of the prisoners was none other than Mr Justice Hardinge, who, two years later, was to preside over Mary Morgan's trial. He was sent from Westminster to attend Great Sessions on the south-eastern circuit twice a year, in spring and autumn. It was his duty to preside over the more serious cases whilst Quarter Sessions were held four times a year where more minor offences were dealt with by justices appointed within each county. The Great Sessions* at Presteigne began on Monday, 8 April 1805 at The Shire Hall, but Mary's case was not heard until three o'clock the following afternoon.

Though Mary's crime—the killing of a bastard child—was commonplace amongst the poor, the attitude of her judge and the effect her ultimate execution had on his conscience was quite remarkable. Although she had suffered months of confinement, (she passed her seventeenth birthday in jail), she emerged from her cell far from downcast, and as she stood in the dock and faced her accusers 'her countenance was pretty and modest; it had even the air and expression of perfect innocence. Not a tear escaped her when all around were deeply affected by her doom; yet her carriage was respectful, her look attentive, serious and intelligent.' So wrote Hardinge to the Bishop of St Asaph the following year.

It was clear from Mary's composure that she fully expected young Wilkins who, either by sheer coincidence or design, had been selected as one of the jurors, to persuade the judge to deal

---

* Changed in 1830 to the Assizes when Wales came within the English circuit system. County Magistrates dealt witrh the General Sessions.

George Hardinge (1744-1816)—Visitor to Maeswyllch Castle
and judge at the trial of Mary Morgan
Son of Nicholas Hardinge, writer and antiquary. Solicitor General to
Queen Victoria, counsel to East India Company and Attorney General.
Had his major speeches printed and distributed and had two books
published: *Letters to Burke on the Impeachment of Hastings* and
The Essence of Malone

with her case with leniency. Indeed, she had said quite openly that she expected him to write a letter to the judge on her behalf.

As George Hardinge was a frequent visitor to Maesllwych when travelling as circuit judge—and had probably seen the pretty young kitchen maid on a number of occasions—it was quite understandable that Mary could never have imagined that her trial would end in a sentence of death. In addition, she may have heard through the grapevine that only a few days before this same judge had been in Brecon presiding over the trial of another young girl, Mary Morris, from Hay; she had also killed her bastard child, cut it up with a pair of scissors and buried it in the garden of a house in Brecon where she was in service. She was acquitted of the charge of murder of the child but was sentenced to two years imprisonment for concealing its birth. And so, with her looks, previous good conduct and air of innocence she must have felt optimistic, especially faced with a Judge who was renowned for his appreciation of pretty women.

But if Walter Wilkins did speak up in her favour his entreaties were made in private and in vain, for having heard the evidence of the cook, the under cook and the dairymaid concerning the birth and its gory sequel, the jury delivered a verdict of 'Guilty'. Despite the severity of his opinions on the crime of infanticide, the judge was visibly moved as he embarked on an emotional speech directed at Mary. His tone was censorious and grave:

'Mary Morgan upon evidence which leaves not the shade of doubt upon the mind, you are convicted of murdering your child...the offspring of your secret and vicious love...'

Though clearly affected by his task the judge continued to speak at great length, at one point telling Mary: 'To cut off a young creature like you in the morning of her day, for it is a little more than a day to the oldest of us all, is an affliction thrown upon me which I have no power to describe, or to bear so well as perhaps I should.... You must not think we are cruel, it is to save other infants like yours and many other girls like you from the pit into which you are fallen.'

When he passed the sentence of death the court witnessed the astonishing spectacle of the judge weeping openly. The sentence stated that the execution was to be carried out within forty-eight hours, which reduced the possibility of a reprieve.* In addition Hardinge ordered that Mary's body be dissected and anatomised.

And so, according to a contemporary account, Mary was taken through the streets to Gallow's Lane on the back of a cart. Dressed in white, her hair loose down her back, she was barely conscious by the time she was dragged to the tree and hanged. It is said that she was so emaciated after six months in gaol that a man was made to pull on her legs to ensure her neck was broken. He was paid a shilling for his efforts. Such was the anger felt by many of the local people that few had joined the crowds that gathered to watch the execution; they chose instead to demonstrate their feelings of repugnance by putting up the shutters on their shops and houses.

Determined to spare Mary the final ignomy of dismemberment some of her supporters removed her body from the tree and buried it in the garden of the Rectory. This garden has since become part of the graveyard of St Andrew's Church, so despite her execution, her remains now lie in consecrated ground, marked by two tomb-stones. The first, and the larger of the two, donated by the Earl of Aylesbury, is inscribed with the words of George Hardinge:

To the memory of Mary Morgan who young and beautiful, endowed with a good understanding and disposition but unen-lightened by the sacred truths of Christianity, became the victim of sin and shame and was condemned to an ignominious death on the 11th April 1805 for the Murder of her bastard Child. Roused to a first sense of guilt and remorse by the eloquent and humane exertions of her benevolent judge Mr Justice Hardinge, she under-went the Sentence of the Law on the following Thursday with unfeigned repentance and a fervent hope of forgiveness through the merits of a redeeming intercessor. This stone is erected not merely to perpetuate the remembrance of a departed penitent, but to remind the living of the frailty of human nature when unsup-ported by religion.

* According to W.H. Howse in his book *The History of Presteigne*, published in 1945, Mary was granted a reprieve but the messenger, sent from London on horseback, arrived too late to save her.

The second, much smaller stone, erected by the people of Presteigne, is thus inscribed:

In memory of Mary Morgan who suffered
April 13th 1805 aged 17 years
He that is without sin among you
Let him first cast the stone at her
The 18th chapter of St John
part of the 7th verse.

Such is the sentiment reserved for young Mary Morgan that every Christmas and on the anniversary of her death, fresh flowers are placed on her grave. And such was George Hardinge's morbid preoccupation with his part in her execution that, as if to justify himself, he wrote this extraordinary letter to the Bishop of St Asaph soon after Mary's death:

The Right Reverend Dr Horseley,
Lord Bishop of St Asaph.   April 1805

My Dear Lord,
With many apologies, and with trembling hope that you will honour the enclosed with your attention, I lay them before you and have nothing more at heart than to obtain a few hints from you upon so awful and so alarming a subject. In our part of Wales it is thought no crime to kill a bastard child. We had two cases equally desperate. One of the culprits (and perhaps the worst of the two in a moral view) escaped. In the case of the girl at Presteigne, circumstances transpired which are of a most affecting and peculiar nature. Her countenance was pretty and modest; it had even the air and expression of perfect innocence. Not a tear escaped from her when all around were deeply affected by her doom; yet her carriage was respectful, her look attentive, serious and intelligent. Short as the interval before she perished, her use of it was most wonderful. It appeared that she had no defect of understanding and that she was born with every disposition to virtue, but of her crime she had not the faintest conception; and there was not a single trace of religion to be found in her

thoughts. Of Christianity she had never even heard, or of the Bible, and she scarce had ever been at church.

A servant in a most profligate family [she] attracted the attention of her young master, who was intrigued with her. Her office was that of undercook and she killed her child the moment after its birth with a penknife, nearly severing the head from the neck. It was the same knife and the same use of it, which had been her implement and constant habit in killing chickens. This murder it appears by her confession (the most ingenious and complete imaginable) that she committed in mercy to her child. The young Squire, though her favourite gallant, was not the father of the child; but she did him justice in reporting that when he was apprized of her pregnancy he offered to maintain the child when born if she would only say that he was the father. Such was her sense of honour, that although it would have saved her child's life and her own, she would not purchase these two lives with a falsehood.

The father of the child before its birth (admitting the fact) refused in pre-emptory terms to maintain it when born. I determined therefore to kill it, poor thing (she said), out of the way, being perfectly sure that I could not provide for it myself.... Before she was tried, she solicited her young master's help in the gift of a single guinea to her, for a Counsel to do the best for her that he could but her prayer was refused and she would have been undefended if the High Sheriff himself had not, in compassion to her desolate situation, fee'd Counsel himself. She took it for granted that she would be acquitted; had ordered gay apparel to attest her deliverance and supposed the young gentleman (whom well I knew) would save her by a letter to me. She embraced the Gospel Creed and its mercies with enlightened as well as fervent hope; took the sacrament with exemplary devotion; marked a perfect sense of remorse and met her fate in a most affecting manner, with calm intrepidity and with devout resignation. The Minister who attended her told me that a feather of religion would have made an Angel of this girl. To wind up the Characters in this Provincial Tragedy, through to the end of her life she spoke with romantic affection of her young master (whom yet she indirectly accused of seducing her) when she was no more, he gave the lie to all she had asserted and without a shadow of interest. It must not be forgot that her fellow servant, the father of the child, when she complained of her sufferings from pregnancy, gave her a herb which he told her that he had gathered and advised her to take it; which she would never do, believing that it was intended by him to kill her child in her womb. As the law stands, concealment of a pregnancy and birth is punished with two years imprisonment at the most though it is in that concealment that all these murders originate. I have never heard of a Divine, Philosopher, Statesman, Judge, Moralist or even Poet who who has written professedly upon this topic. There is, I believe, no illusion to it in Scripture. It never happens in high life, is the vice of the poor, and generally in the pale of domestic servitude....

There has not been a conviction at the Old Bailey for this crime for a period of twenty years and cases of trial for it have been very few. In Wales they have been twice as numerous and very often fatal. In Ireland I am told the habit of exposing children to the elements, most of who die, rages like a pestilence. I wish to have your Lordship's opinion how you would correct the law upon that subject and what expedients you would recommend for prevention of the mischief.....

I remain with the highest respect my Lord,
Your Grateful and Obedient Servant,
George Hardinge

Shortly after his wife died in 1777, the bishop had married her young maidservant, Sarah Wright. As a man who shared his predilection for working class girls the judge may have felt able to unburden his distress on the matter of Mary Morgan. The judge's interest in the Mary Morgan case remained until the end of his life and whenever his duties as Circuit Judge brought him to Presteigne he made a point of visiting her grave.

Over the years since Mary's death there has been a great deal of speculation as to the identity of the father of her bastard child. Was it her fellow servant? Could it be that, as he didn't come forward and support his young mistress he was, in fact, a married man? And did Mary hold out against the abortion he offered her, hoping that he would relent and leave his wife when the child was born?

Or was it, despite Mary's denial, the young Squire, Walter Wilkins, who the girl said offered to maintain it provided she named him as the father—yet who, after her execution, denied that he had been in any way involved with her. But, surely, if the child had been his, its unfortunate death would have been hushed up, the tiny corpse disposed of and no one the wiser. Yet if the child was not his, why was Mary so sure that young Walter would write to the judge on her behalf and ensure her acquittal? Clearly Walter had promised he would—why did he change his mind? Was it more convenient to have her executed and out of the way?

Some have even suggested that Mr Justice Hardinge himself was the father but this is most unlikely—though he may well have sired illegitimate offspring elsewhere—as Circuit Judge he travelled from Westminster to Wales twice yearly—in April and in September. There is no way of determining whether Mary's child was born prematurely or at full term. If her pregnancy had run full term it had begun in January 1804 whilst the Judge was at Westminster. If, however, the child was born at six months— quite possible, to a slight, undernourished, overworked adolescent who had tried to conceal it—Hardinge could have been responsible, the result of his stay at Maesllwych in April 1804. His marriage was childless and the embittered speeches at Mary's trial illustrate the passionate abhorrence he was unable to conceal for the notion that a woman could kill her own child. Would that explain the vicious sentence he gave young Mary and his morbid preoccupation with her after her execution?

Nor did his fascination with Mary Morgan fade. That it continued to prey on his mind is evidenced not only by his visits to the grave, but by several sentimental poems he wrote about her. Indeed, in 1816, eleven years after Mary's death, George Hardinge collapsed whilst at her graveside. Already ill with a severe chest infection he was taken back to his lodgings in the Old Rectory close by. He died of pleurisy a few days later.

Many questions in this sad and unusual case remain unanswered and unless, at some future date, further documentation is found, the identity of the father of Mary's child is destined to remain, as it was then, a secret.

IV

The killing of Silver John

The bizarre tale of the murder of John Lloyd was one familiar to the late eighteenth century locals who regularly drank in the public bar of The Fforest Inn, in the Harley Valley, Radnorshire. It was a story that was told, time and time again, to anyone who would listen. And listen they did, repeatedly, for like all the best stories it contained some truly fascinating ingredients—a kindly, eccentric healer, content with little, who was murdered by men of violence and greed. And it had an extraordinarily chilling ending, for the victim was to reappear in the weirdest circumstances as if to haunt the perpetrators of the crime.

John Lloyd is the central figure in this drama; at the turn of the century he and his family were living on a small farm beneath the frowning brow of Great Graigau and, like most men along this part of the Radnorshire-Herefordshire border, he just managed to scratch a living from his flock of sheep. But it was a hard life and in an era long before the convenience of the motor car, the telephone and a network of veterinary services, small farmers such as Lloyd were totally self-sufficient, their own health and that of their animals, entirely dependent on folk remedies that had been tried and tested for generations.

John Lloyd, however, seemed to have a special gift for healing. He attended to all the medical needs of the animals in his care and even performed simple surgery. He dispensed all his own medicines and made special poultices using herbs and other natural materials freely at hand. He also became a proficient bone-setter, an enviable skill in such a rugged and isolated area.

37

William Calcraft, public hangman

It soon became common knowledge that John Lloyd was something of an expert and one day he was asked to attend a lad who had broken his leg. He was the son of a miller who lived further down the valley, at Haines Mill. So successful was Lloyd in neatly setting the bone that the grateful miller offered to pay him for his services. Surprisingly, John Lloyd refused to take any money but, when pressed, agreed to accept two silver buttons instead.

It was the fashion for gentlemen of the day to exhibit their wealth by dressing their top coats with silver buttons. These were not dainty decorations but large, heavy discs of solid silver and worth a considerable sum. It would appear that John Lloyd decided to emulate this habit, starting in a less ostentatious way with his waistcoat. Over the years, Lloyd's reputation as a healer and bonesetter grew and, although he worked wonderfully on the shattered limbs of men and animals, he never deviated from his refusal to take money. His collection of silver tokens increased accordingly and before long his waistcoat was covered with silver buttons, testimony to both his skill and the gratitude of his patients. When every available inch of fabric was covered he began to pin his precious buttons to his overcoat instead. And to match his bizarre appearance and legendary skill he soon acquired the nickname of 'Silver John'.

Most of Lloyd's clients were neighbouring hill-farmers but at one time he treated Sir William de Breos, a gentleman of Norman descent, who lived at Tomen Castle. When he broke his ankle he sent for Lloyd, anxious to avoid the possible legacy of such a complicated fracture—a crippled foot. Greatly relieved with the outcome he rewarded Lloyd with a pair of silver shoe buckles.

Yet more successes followed for Silver John. Nor did he confine himself to healing human beings—after all a broken bone is a broken bone and when the parson's hunter broke its ankle John Lloyd was called in to help. For his services, once again, Lloyd refused to accept money but was happy to receive a silver snuff-box instead. His reward for yet another act of healing was a silver-knobbed walking stick which became as much a hallmark as his clothes which were now drooping under the weight of all his silver buttons. Far too busy to do it himself, the tedious task of polishing them all fell to his son and namesake, John.

So cumbersome had his coat become that he took to wearing it only on special occasions, such as on his regular trips to Builth Market to buy and sell sheep. He also insisted on wearing it whenever he was treating patients, human or animal. One wonders whether the aim was to instil confidence, rather like a doctor's white coat, or whether it was a subtle reminder to the recipient that a silver token of some kind would be much appreciated.

Fairs and markets were a great feature of rural life in the eighteenth and nineteenth centuries, not just for the serious business of trading livestock, hiring labour and exchanging gossip but also for entertainment. The lives of most rural workers were marked by hardship and deprivation and the Hiring Fairs, usually held twice yearly, and coinciding with pay-days, were occasions where a certain amount of over-indulgence and high spirits were often the order of the day.

It was whilst returning late at night from the Michaelmas Fair at Builth Wells in his horse-drawn gambo—a flat, two wheeled Welsh cart—that Silver John met his fate. Somewhere, between the market place and his home in the hills, he was waylaid and mercilessly slaughtered. Familiar with the country lanes and mountain tracks, the horse continued on the homeward journey, arriving at the Lloyd's farm pulling an empty cart, which bore no clue as to the old man's disappearance.

As the days and weeks passed without sight of Silver John his family and friends must have resigned themselves to the possibility that something sinister had happened to him. As indeed it had. But the mystery was soon to be solved. It was early in the following year, probably 1789, which was a particularly bad winter, that the nearby stretch of water called Llynhylin, was frozen over, forming a large, solid ice-rink. The villagers decided that this would make an unusual venue for the Radnor Candlemas Fair. As the younger revellers skated around the ice, clutching each other and fooling around, others feasted on specially made cake and hot cider. The light from the fires that had been lit around the edge of the water added an almost magical quality to the scene.

But the atmosphere was set to change. One minute, young Mary, (whose father was landlord of The Fforest Inn), was happily skating on the far side of the lake with her friend—the next, she suddenly slipped and fell face downwards onto the ice. Her cry came not from the indignity of the fall or from any injury, but so loud and terrible was her scream that it was easily heard above the laughter and singing of the villagers. They ran towards her, fearful of what they might find.

But nothing could have prepared them for what they saw. Mary, her hand covering her ashen face and hardly daring to look, pointed towards her feet. There, preserved and encased in the ice, like some terrible spectre in a Horror Film, was the mutilated face of 'Silver John'.

Horrified, the villagers debated what to do—how were they to pull the body free of the ice without breaking it up? It was a gruesome dilemma but it was eventually decided to wait until there was a thaw so that Silver John's body could be lifted from the water intact and then properly buried. It wasn't until a thaw several weeks later that this could be done.

And it was only then that his friends knew for certain how 'Silver John' had died. He hadn't, as the less charitable had imagined, had too much to drink at the Fair and fallen into the lake on his way home. It was clear he had been murdered and robbery seemed to be the most likely motive, for his coat, covered with silver buttons, was missing. Gone, too, were his silver-topped cane and his snuff-box and the silver buckles had been callously ripped from his shoes.

Worse still, if a local rhyme bears any element of truth, his eyes were also missing:

> Silver John is dead and gone,
> So they came home a-singing.
> Radnor boys pulled out his eyes
> And set the bells a-ringing.

This last act of brutality was probably done to obliterate the murderer's image which, folklore would have it, remained forever imprinted on the retina of the victim.

A great crowd followed Silver John's coffin, borne on his old gambo, up the Harley Valley, where he was buried on the slopes of Great Graigau. Many of the mourners were grateful patients, able to walk and earn their livings because of his kindness and skill. One cannot help wondering whether his murderers were, indeed, local Radnor people, who, anxious not to be noticed by their absence, joined the procession up the mountain that day— and whether, during the long winter evenings round the fire at The Fforest Inn, they had to listen in silence, time and time again, as some local raconteur told of the murder of Silver John.

V

Feuding Farmers

Life for the hill farmer has always been hard, never more so than in the early nineteenth century. Of the few recorded cases of murder, at least on the Welsh side of the border, these were often the result of disputes over territory or long-standing feuds—the origins of which were at times barely remembered. Such acts of violence, commonly sparked off by fairly innocuous events, were often the culmination of past provocation, resentment and ill-feeling that had been allowed to fester and finally explode.

One such case, in 1807, was that of the Powell family from Foxhall Farm and the Williamses from Twyn, both sheep farmers in the Llanbedr hills. Their long-standing feud came to a head when William Williams, known as Billy the Twyn, had given evidence before the magistrates at Crickhowell, against his neighbour, Thomas Powell, for stealing one of his sheep. Rather than reimburse Williams for the missing sheep as required by the court, Thomas Powell absconded until the matter died down. His wife, Anne, together with their sons, Timothy and John, and daughter Sarah, lay the blame for his absence on Billy the Twyn. Undoubtedly, it caused his family hardship—to the sum of £100 according to his son, John—and the resentment felt against their neighbour became so intense that when Billy the Twyn was found dead, the whole Powell family stood trial for his murder.

When questioned before the magistrates during the initial inquiry, Mary Richmond, a maid-of-all work in the Powell household, said that a few days before the murder she heard her mistress discussing her husband's disappearance and it was obvious that the family intended to get even with Billy the Twyn. Questioned further she said that about a fortnight before the murder John had returned to the house about 7 o'clock in the evening. When his mother asked him why he was so late he said that while he was working in the fields he'd met the hated Billy the Twyn, who'd had the cheek to ask him to pay for the stolen sheep. Billy had his two sons with him, otherwise, said John, he would have had a real fight on his hands.

At the subsequent inquest, the maid was asked to give a full account of the day of the murder. She said that in the morning Thomas Powell, having returned to the farm, was eating breakfast with his wife, sons and daughter at 10 o'clock. Half an hour later she had gone with John to plough one of the fields above the house. She saw Billy the Twyn and his two sons about 12 o'clock talking to another farmer; a little later she saw Billy coursing some sheep near the Powells' land.

About this time Timothy arrived with some refreshments and warned his brother about Billy being in the area. He then tried to persuade John to take a break and go back to the house, where presumably his mother and sister were preparing the mid-day meal. But John was content to carry on with the ploughing. Later he and Mary saw Timothy and Billy the Twyn obviously engaged in some sort of 'cat and mouse' game along the boundary between the two farms. Timothy was crouching behind the hedge near one of their fields, as though he was spying on Billy the Twyn. When John called to him to drive out a cow that had wandered into the next field, Timothy jumped over the hedge with a large stick in his hand, and went after the animal.

A few minutes later, Mary recalled seeing Billy the Twyn walking towards the spot near the hedge where Timothy had been hiding. He also jumped over the hedge and walked towards a copse in the Powells' field. The next thing Mary saw was Billy the Twyn following Timothy into the woods—possibly to ask him yet again for the money owed to him. Still working at the plough, the servant girl then saw Timothy in the field beyond the woods and watched him go towards the farmhouse. He was alone and there was no sign of Billy the Twyn.

A quarter of an hour later Timothy came back to the field where she and John Powell were working. She noticed that his face was very pale and he kept looking at his hands. Passing her without speaking he went over to his brother and, after whispering something in his ear, pointed towards the wood. Then she and the two brothers returned to the house where Timothy ate some food and changed his clothes. He also got John to cut his hair for him before going to the well to wash.

Once back inside the house he talked quietly to his brother and then 'took a bundle of shoes and went away on the road to Llanbedr.' Mary did not see him again until he was arrested and charged with murder.

The body of Billy the Twyn was found by his wife, Anne, and his son, William, between 10 and 11 o'clock the next morning in the wood on the Powells' farm. He was lying 'concealed under a holly-bush lying with his face downwards'. He was 'dead and cold, and wounded and bloody'. It was later established that he died of blows to the head; his hat was never found.

At the subsequent trial the account of Timothy Powell's arrest on the Sunday after the murder was given by William Walter of Llanbedr. He had seen him leaving the Powell farm between 3 and 4 o'clock on the day of the murder, carrying a bundle under his arm. The following evening, about 11, he and some friends went looking for Timothy at the house of Phoebe Jones, possibly a girl friend, at Cwmbanw. They told her that he was suspected of murder and then asked if he was inside. By way of reply the woman gave them a candle and told them to search for him themselves. Then, in a voice loud enough to carry through the unplastered ceiling to the floor above, she said: 'Timothy, come down, and God forbid you are guilty.'

William Walter met Timothy at the top of the narrow staircase and seized him by the collar and, with the help of one William Bowen, took him to a lodging house for the night. On the way there was a struggle but although all three men fell to the ground, others came to their assistance and prevented Timothy's escape. The following day there was no shortage of volunteers to frogmarch him to the magistrates' court at Crickhowell. Meanwhile, others had arrested his brother, John; an entry in the Quarter Sessions Book of Orders for Brecon testifies to their efforts: 'Ordered that the thanks of his Court be transmitted by the Clerk of the Peace to Capt John Brookwood and the volunteers of Crickhowell for their readiness and alacrity in assisting the civil powers in apprehending John Powell and Timothy Powell committed to the county gaol for the murder of William Williams.'

Although the whole Powell family were eventually arrested and charged with the murder of their sworn enemy, Billy the Twyn, only Timothy was found guilty as charged. He was duly sentenced to death by public hanging, an event recorded with a grievous additional note by the reporter for *The Cambrian* newspaper:

'On Monday, Timothy Powell was executed pursuant to his sentence. On that morning he attempted to strangle himself by tying a silk handkerchief round his neck and fastening it to the iron bars of the grating to the door of his cell. This miserable creature died as he lived, obdurate, resentful and apparently impenitent.'

* * *

A similar feud plagued the lives of two other hill farming families in Llanafan-fawr, in 1826. Rees Lewis and his neighbour John Price, were both small farmers and had been quarrelling for many years, possibly over grazing rights.* Rees Lewis kept his sheep on three grazing areas—Vanfed, Bryn-rhydd and Lan-goch. John Price did the same only he also kept some stock on another hill-side called the Darren.

One Sunday morning John Price and his son, Peter, met Rees Lewis on the Vanfed hill. According to Peter a row soon broke

---

* In the late 17th century a father and son, related to Rees Lewis, had been hanged for killing a neighbour as part of a long-standing feud over territory.

out and he saw Rees Lewis waving a stick at his father and swearing that he would be sorry for whatever it was he had done. The two men had reached the point where they could no longer remain civil and arguments flared up whenever their paths crossed.

On Sunday, 23 April, Price and his son went up the Darren hill at about four o'clock in the morning. They had already been up to Vanfed and Bryn-rhydd and seen Rees Lewis and his son, David, there. A little later Rees Lewis left his son on the hill saying he was going home for some breakfast. But about this time Price's son, Peter, was surprised to see him on the slopes of the Darren. There seemed no reason for him being there as he never grazed sheep on that particular hillside. On his way down to the farm for his own breakfast at about 8 o'clock Peter met his father going back to the hills; it must have been at this point that the two feuding farmers met and resumed their previous argument. After going down to attend chapel Peter went home for his mid-day meal but did not see his father. In the afternoon, between 1 and 2 o'clock, on his way back to the Darren, he looked across and saw Rees Lewis on Bryn-rhydd, with, he was sure, a stick in his hand. When he reached the Darren hill Peter found the body of his father; although he was lying with his face downwards he could see that it was swollen and bloodied. He also found that his father's handkerchief was tied so tightly around his neck that he couldn't get his fingers underneath to loosen it. He realised that his father had been strangled.

Shocked, Peter ran home to fetch help. James Jones, the parish constable was informed and, with the help of friends, the body of John Price was carried down the hillside to the farmhouse. On hearing about the long-standing feud between the dead man and Rees Lewis, the constable hurried to the Lewis farm by which time Rees had already fled. Some days later he was arrested by a labourer from Lanafan-fawr called John Williams who came across Rees, looking weak and wretched, on a footpath. Recognising him as the wanted man, he grabbed his collar and frog-marched him, apparently with little resistance, to the house of Rees Davies, another constable at Penrhiw-moch.

During his subsequent trial for the murder of John Price, a number of witnesses were called, one being the wife of a stone-mason, Elizabeth Davies, who lived in a cottage at Llanafan-fawr, opposite Rees Lewis's farm. She had been feeling unwell on the afternoon of the murder and was lying down—she could see the Lewis' house from her bed and swore that, about three o'clock that Sunday afternoon, she saw Rees Lewis run from his house, climb over a stile and disappear across the fields, obviously agitated and in a hurry.

Although Rees Lewis appeared calm during most of his trial when his thirteen year old son, David, was called as a witness for the prosecution, he became agitated. The lad had originally been imprisoned in Brecon gaol for 15 weeks on suspicion of being his father's accomplice but had since been released. Seeing his son about to testify against him, Rees seemed genuinely upset and sorrowfully shook his head. His wife, seated close by, did the same, as though warning the boy not to say anything that would harm his father's case. Although David, lacking in even the most fundamental schooling, was illiterate, he seemed determined to tell the truth. He said he had gone with his father to Vanfed and Bryn-rhydd after their breakfast on the day of the murder. His father had left him there while he went to look for three sheep that had strayed that morning. He fell asleep and only woke two hours later when his father returned, asking if he had any blood on his face. There was, indeed, a small speck of blood near his eye. Frightened, the boy had refused to wipe it off when asked so Rees did it himself with a handful of grass.

They returned to the house for their dinner after which Rees asked his son to go back to the hills to watch the sheep but, possibly suspecting that the body of John Price might be lying out there, he said he was too frightened to go. He was eventually persuaded to ride the mare and met James Jones, the constable, already on his way to the spot where Price's body had been found. When he rode back home his father had already left.

Although there were several witnesses willing to testify to Rees Lewis's good character the evidence against him, though purely circumstantial, was certainly damning. Further credence was given to his guilt when a prisoner from Brecon gaol, one David Morris, recalled a conversation he'd had with Rees Lewis whilst in prison awaiting trial. Lewis had, he said, more or less admitted killing Price, at the same time boasting that his guilt could not be proved as nobody had seen him do it. The jury, having listened to the Chief Justice's summing up, took fifteen minutes to declare the prisoner guilty. He was sentenced to death for his crime and duly executed on Monday, 14 August, before a huge crowd that had gathered outside Brecon gaol to watch him hang.

Prior to his death Rees Lewis confessed his guilt and acknowledged the justice of his sentence. He admitted that all the witnesses had spoken truthfully except the prisoner who said he'd confessed during a conversation while awaiting trial. For some reason, he denied that this conversation ever took place. The reason for the long-standing feud between Rees Lewis and John Price is not known nor what exactly happened to spark off that final, disastrous explosion of anger that resulted in the death of both.

* * *

Hardship seemed to have contributed to the death of a farm-worker, Thomas Edwards, in November 1848. The scene of the crime was a hill farm close to the Brecon Beacons, two miles from the town of Brecon itself. It was customary for farmers in the area to pay their labourers and household servants twice yearly—at the time of the Hiring Fairs. The main ones were held in May and November and as this was the only time the workers had any money, new clothes were the order of the day. Those who had been laid off would present themselves for hire, spruced up and sporting perhaps a new jacket or pair of boots. It is said that farm lads would stand close to the cattle pens, where the farmers were congregated, with a straw hanging from the corner of their mouths as a sign that they were available for hire. Housemaids would advertise themselves by wearing their aprons, removing them once they had found someone to employ them. Once this had been achieved they were free to enjoy the fair and frequent the rowdy ale-houses packed solid with revellers. It was a great day out for the youngsters many of whom were in hard, menial jobs with little time for fun. It was also a chance for the lads to cut a dash with the girls, most of whom were in domestic service and rarely allowed out.

James Griffiths was an eighteen year old itinerant worker with very little money. He had been taken on as a temporary labourer, for three weeks only, at 3/- a week, by John Powell, at his farm at Cwmgwdi. But when the three weeks were up he agreed to stay for a further week. According to John Powell, Griffiths seemed troubled when the fourth week was up and, as he was a likeable lad and a good worker, he let him stay until the next Hiring Fair. But he made it clear that he would have to go at the November Fair as he could not afford to employ him for the winter. To tide him over until then, Powell's wife gave him 4/6 but a little later James Griffiths asked Powell to advance him a further 7/- or 8/- so he could buy a pair of trousers for the fair. But the farmer refused saying he would have to wait as he was not prepared to hand over money not yet earned.

On the Saturday, a week before the Brecon fair Powell paid his permanent labourer Thomas Edwards 30/- wages. James wasn't given any money, and although he didn't repeat his request for a loan, Powell took pity on him and gave him 2/-. He intended to pay the remaining 7/- when the lad was due to leave on 17 November. That day James Griffiths and Thomas Edwards had started work in the stables at their usual time of five o'clock in the morning. John Powell was to say later:

'On Friday, November 17, I was called up about 6.30, and with Elizabeth Philips, [the maid], my son, daughter, and wife, I went to the dunghill, and at the foot of the dunghill I found Thomas Edwards. He was nearly doubled up with his head near his knees and assisted by the others I carried him into the house. He was in a dreadful state, his head and face being covered with blood. Seeing him in a dying condition I sent my son for Mr North, the

50

surgeon at Brecon. Mr Probert, a blacksmith, came later and with him I went out to search. We found a pitchfork which had blood on it in two places corresponding to the hands of a man. I kept it in my possession until the inquest and gave it to Richard Beard, the constable. Whilst going to the chaffroom I knocked against Thomas Edwards's hat, which had a hole in it. I kept the hat in the house and gave it to Richard Beard at the examination before the magistrates with some other things. On the same morning after it was daylight I went again to examine the dunghill. Beard, the constable, was with me. The heap seemed to have been stirred about and we found some blood near the foot of it.... On showing the place to two gentlemen from Brecon the next day I found a piece of skull. When I found him, deceased was able to utter a few detached sentences, but he was not sensible....'

Powell's wife, Mary, had helped to carry Thomas Edwards into the house and nursed him throughout the day. It was she who then found the murder weapon, a blood-stained axe, partially immersed in water in the gutter. Her daughter, Janet, had used it to chop wood at about 4 o'clock the day before and instead of returning it to its usual place in the back kitchen she had left it in the block in the rick-yard.

Mr North, the surgeon from Brecon, arrived at 7.30 that morning. Finding Thomas Edwards semi-conscious on the settle near the fire he had him removed to bed and his head shaved. He found that a five inch square area of the poor man's skull had been badly smashed. Having managed to remove some twenty four pieces of broken bone he stayed with his patient until 10.30 a.m. When he called again in the afternoon, not surprisingly, Thomas Edwards was still in a terrible state and died a few hours later.

Although young James Griffiths had run away soon after the murder he was eventually tracked down and arrested in Suffolk. In all probability his family were living there, though he may simply have fled as far from the scene of the crime as he could, seeking labouring jobs on the way. John Powell was sent for and at Ipswich gaol he identified the lad, saying: 'Well, James, little did I think you would have done such a thing in my house. I am

William Calcraft was hangman from 1829-74,
longer than any other man. As he aged, so he became clumsy
and rarely administered a clean death

sorry to see you in such a place.' James, it seems, simply 'hung
his head and made no reply.'

The trial of James Griffiths was held at the Brecon Spring
Assizes of 1849, presided over by Mr Justice Erle. Charged with
the murder of Thomas Edwards he entered a plea of not guilty
but, regrettably, there was no one to speak in his defence. After
listening to all the witnesses and the judge's summing up, the jury
only took ten minutes to find James Griffiths guilty as charged.
The judge clearly agreed with their verdict for, on sentencing
Griffiths, he said:

'James Griffiths, you stand convicted by a jury of an aggravated wilful murder. I have carefully attended to the evidence and

feel bound to state that it leaves no doubt in my mind that the verdict is right. It appears to me that you had planned your crime with calmness and deliberation. You had made preparations for carrying into effect your awful design. You had prepared the dreadful weapon and thus planned the death of a man who was your friendly companion. You had likewise planned and contrived a way in which to conceal your guilt by covering the corpse, and all this appears to have been done for the purpose of getting possession of his property. By Divine and human law the punishment of death is reward for the crime of murder. So far as it rests with me the law will take its course. I therefore exhort you to implore your Heavenly Redeemer, and pray for that mercy which is denied you in this world.'

While the judge was speaking James Griffiths, the picture of wretchedness and remorse, sat with his head against the front of the dock, a handkerchief over his face.

A few days later the streets of Brecon were once more swarming with people, this time anxious to watch James Griffiths die in front of Brecon County gaol. The notorious Newgate executioner, William Calcraft, had travelled early that morning from London to carry out the sentence of death. Shortly before 10 a.m. he escorted James Griffiths to the scaffold. The lad declined his right to address the huge crowd, keeping his head down and his eyes averted. As in so many cases of this kind, the deplorable fact is that he did not die instantaneously from a broken neck—he squirmed convulsively on the rope for some four minutes after the bolt was drawn, until he died, not from dislocation of the neck, but from strangulation.

One can only guess at young Griffiths's reasons for smashing the skull of his workmate, a man with whom, it was said, he was on friendly terms. Had he, perhaps, misunderstood the situation when John Powell had paid him the 2/-, not realising that he fully intended to pay him the remaining 7/- on the day his employment ended, the day of the murder? Did his resentment reach boiling point when he saw Powell hand over 30/- to Thomas Edwards? Was he so desperate for some money to buy clothes before the Hiring Fair the next day that he was prepared to kill for it? And was there, one wonders, a young girl he wished to take to the fair and impress with a new outfit? And did Thomas Edwards drive him mad with frustration by refusing to lend him any money— and did that frustration drive him to kill—for the price of a pair of trousers?

VI

The Murderous Young Highwayman

By the beginning of the nineteenth century the rapid increase in population had resulted in the development of a number of fair-sized towns in the Welsh valleys. As these communities were still largely dependent upon smallholders from outlying districts for their vegetables, meat and dairy produce, rural traders would trek from town to town selling their wares. As these journeys were often long and arduous, the carriers, who enjoyed a camaraderie similar to that of the long distance lorry drivers of today, would often stop overnight at various cheap hostelries en route.

David Lewis, the victim of a murderous young highwayman, was one such man—a butter merchant from Lampeter. Very late on the night of 6 December, 1843, John Lewis, keeper of the turnpike known as Trecastle Eastern Gate, was disturbed by the sound of crying. On going out to investigate he found a boy standing alone at the gate, in charge of two horse-drawn carts. He had come from the direction of Brecon and was crying miserably, saying that he didn't have any money to pay the toll. The keeper took the lad into the toll-house but, about three quarters of an hour later, he was disturbed by some waggoners travelling to Llandovery. One of the men, Evan Evans, speaking to the boy in Welsh, discovered that his father was missing. They had been travelling together, he said, and had somehow become separated. After a while, both Evan Evans, and his companion, Morgan Morgan, continued on their way.

The toll keeper decided to take the unfortunate lad to the inn at Trecastle until his father could be found but before they got far one of the waggoners came galloping back saying a man had been found dead on the road whom he suspected was the boy's father. He guided the keeper and the boy to the site and the latter saw straight away that it was indeed the body of his father.

The parish constable was roused from his bed at three o'clock that morning and arranged for the body to be taken to the Three Horses Inn at Trecastle. On making his search of the dead man he found a fob watch, a knife and a button in one of the trouser pockets; as well as a memorandum book and a new silk handkerchief—but no money.

When a surgeon, Mr Daniel Gyngel, was called to examine the body the only sign of injury was a wound above the man's right ear from which he extracted a bullet. On examining the man's hat he found a hole that corresponded exactly with the entry of the bullet that had clearly killed him. When the boy was questioned he revealed that he was twelve years old and his name was David Lewis—the same as his father. They had left their home at Tanfforest, near Lampeter, on the previous Monday with two carts loaded with casks of butter. Some of this was sold on their way through the Brecon hills and he had seen money exchanged.

It was while they were returning through Brecon that the boy's father called at the barracks, presumably to sell butter. As the boy waited outside another carrier called Thomas Thomas accosted him and asked him who was the owner of the carts. When his father reappeared they made their way to the Bridgend Inn, to sell butter and get some refreshment. By the time they eventually left Brecon it was getting dark so Lewis lit a lantern which he attached to the shaft of the first cart, in which the boy was riding. About three miles out of the town they drew alongside another wagon, in which Thomas Thomas had hitched a ride. Jumping down, Thomas fell in with David Lewis as he walked behind with the second cart. As the journey continued the two men and the boy took turns at driving the lead cart and walking, partly to keep warm as the night air had grown cold.

After a while the lad huddled under a tarpaulin in the second cart and fell asleep. He last saw his father and Thomas Thomas walking together behind the cart, chatting quite amicably. He did not wake up until the horses stopped at Trecastle toll-gate where he realised his father was missing.

As soon as he heard about the murder of David Lewis, and the son's description of his father's last known companion, David Prosser, the landlord of The Bridgend Inn in Brecon, felt certain that the murderer must be Thomas Thomas. He straight away alerted the parish constable and the arrest of twenty-four year old Thomas soon followed. It was described by the superintendent of rural police in Carmarthenshire, Mr Enoch Gwynne:

'I had been in pursuit of the prisoner. I saw him on the day previous to receiving instructions to apprehend him. I then made for his father's house and met him on a bridge. I then seized hold of him. He struggled and threw me down on the ground. I drew my cutlass and told him if he did not surrender I would be obliged to use it. He rose his hands and I suspected he threw something away. When we got close to the Black Lion I called on policeman Thomas to open the door, when prisoner threw himself on his back, put his hand in his breast pocket and dropped something. I asked Thomas to go and see what it was. He went out, called me to the door, and pointed to two pistols which were on the ground. Neither was loaded. I then searched the prisoner and found in his pocket twelve balls, gunpowder in two papers, mould and key, the mould corresponding with the balls.'

A search of Thomas Thomas's home also produced a number of banknotes and two cheques thought to have been stolen from the murdered butter merchant. Thomas was formally charged with the murder of David Lewis and sent for trial at Brecon Assizes on 24 March, 1845. According to *The Carmarthen Journal*, 'the unhallowed ground where the fearful murder was committed is marked by a small heap of stones through which protrudes a delicate shrub which shows the promise of luxuriance'. The reporter goes on to regret that 'so lovely a spot should be desecrated by so foul an act'.

It was not until Tuesday, 25 March, 1845, that the case against Thomas Thomas was opened at Brecon Town Hall before Mr Justice Cresswell, who, right at the start of the proceedings, expressed his regret that the case had occasioned so much controversy and gossip in the area. This, he felt, 'greatly lessened the chance of an unbiased hearing'. As it was the first capital offence to be tried in Brecon for eighteen years 'the various avenues leading to the Town Hall were quite blocked up for a considerable period previous to the opening of the doors.' The crowd was so dense that 'barristers, attorneys, reporters and others who attended on business could not affect an entrance to court without the greatest of difficulty'.

In fact, the clamouring of the thwarted crowds grew to such a crescendo that they were allowed into the passageway leading to the Court so that Mr Chilton, for the prosecution, could be heard inside.' As soon as the doors of the county hall were opened 'a rush took place and the crowd entered pell mell and every accessible spot was at once occupied. The solemnity of the proceedings, however, was felt and the very miscellaneous crowd conducted themselves with gravity befitting the occasion. The accommodation of the bench itself was taxed to make room for the numerous ladies, the body of which constituted the largest proportion of the audience, a circumstance which his Lordship significantly alluded to as not the most feminine exhibition in the world.' Mr Justice Cresswell was not the first, nor the last judge to view with disdain the fact that women seemed particularly fascinated by murder trials. That the prisoner's youth and good looks might have inspired part of their interest appears not to have occurred to him.

When charged the prisoner replied 'Not Guilty' in a voice that trembled with 'emotion and apprehension'. A reporter remarked: 'The prisoner is in the 24th year of the age and as he stood in the dock gazing on the crowd of upturned faces that were directed on his in one burning focus, he exhibited the appearance of a man on whom apprehension and anxiety had done their work and by anticipation afforded a practical illustration of the scriptural reproof: "There is no peace for the wicked".'

Another contemporary report described the prisoner as 'dressed in a brown coat, a red plush waistcoat, and a red handkerchief..... he appeared to view all the proceedings with the greatest possible coolness and indifference. There was a perpetual

58

smile kept upon his countenance. It appeared that the prisoner himself was the only unconcerned person present. He nevertheless listened attentively to the proceedings and also ate or drank with avidity whatever the Governor of the Gaol handed him. ... He is about five foot six in height, strong built, and for placidity of expression and regularity of feature, would be pronounced decidedly "well-looking". In his well developed soft blue eye, though occasionally anxious in its expression, and the good-humoured florid cheek, the physiognomist would be at a loss to discover the daring and resolution that connived and perpetrated a murder so diabolical'.

After Mr Chilton, for the prosecution, had given the court a summary of the case before them, David Prosser, the landlord of The Bridgend Inn, was called to give evidence. He said that Thomas had been in his pub that night asking if there were any carriers expected on the road out from Brecon. Thinking his interest was perfectly innocent, in that he merely wanted to secure a lift, he suggested he hurry and catch up with David Lewis and his son, who had just left.

There followed a number of witnesses who could testify that they saw Thomas in various pubs in Brecon and on the highway on the night David Lewis was murdered. Also called to give evidence were various clients to whom Lewis had sold butter in the days prior to his murder; they were able to positively identify the bank notes found at Thomas's house after his arrest. No defence was offered.

The judge began his summing up at half past five 'amid the most profound silence'. He was fair and meticulous in his address and at six o'clock the jury retired. By this time, much of Thomas's confidence had disappeared and, whilst the jurors were out he sat 'sullen and resigned'. He occasionally talked to the chaplain sitting beside him in the dock, but he kept looking towards the door of the jury room. When, half an hour later, the jury returned and announced a verdict of 'Guilty', an eye-witness noticed that 'the shock to the prisoner was perceptible. The confident and assured manner, which he had retained throughout, forsook him, and he gazed about in a bewildered manner.'

When asked if there was anything he wished to say before sentence was passed he remained silent. The judge placed the black cap on his head and began his pronouncement:

'Prisoner at the bar—you have been, after a long, anxious and painful inquiry, found guilty of murder, an inquiry conducted, I am happy to think, on the part of an intelligent jury with every consideration for your position, and exhibiting an anxiety to make themselves acquainted with every part of the case bearing for or against you. I feel bound to say that the evidence detailed was such that no reasonable man who heard your trial could entertain the slightest particle of doubt respecting your guilt.' The prisoner, who had buried his face in his handkerchief, his hands resting on the front of the dock, here lifted up both hands and exclaimed, 'I am not guilty, my Lord'. But the judge replied sternly: 'It is vain for you to say so now; your earthly trial is over; your doom is decided. The last sentence of an earthly judge must be passed upon you. Remember the other world to which you are hastening, and to which, in the painful discharge of my duty I must consign you, another and more awful trial awaits you. Oh, remember that and let the short space you have to live here be spent in penitence and prayer. Your victim was taken up unprepared in the midst of the peaceful pursuits of his honest industry, hurried to his account without any sort of preparation. The law which you have outraged is more merciful to you. Employ, I entreat you, that brief space which is left to you, in seeking for mercy where mercy alone can be found.

'It only remains for me to pronounce upon you the sentence of the law which is that you be carried thence from the place from whence you came and then to a common place of execution where you shall be hanged by the neck until you are dead. Your body will be buried within the precincts of the gaol and may the Lord God Almighty have mercy upon your soul.'

'A slight murmur of applause followed, with clapping of hands, (which the good feeling of the majority soon suppressed instantly), so little sympathy was felt for the prisoner. The unhappy man, who had his face buried in his handkerchief during the passing of the sentence, was led from the dock by the governor of the gaol'.

The public's interest in the prisoner lost none of its fervour, however, and the local press continued to issue bulletins on his behaviour whilst awaiting execution, of which the following are typical:

'His conduct in jail was frequently marked with a recklessness and levity which baffled the curious and which the remonstrances of the Rev. gentlemen in attendance on him could not always control.'

Thomas's truculence was, no doubt, partly caused by fear, as the following extract illustrates:

'The convict, Thomas, at present shews no disposition to confess. He is moody and silent on the subject and the solicitations of the clergymen in attendance on him have had, as yet, little effect. He cried bitterly on entering the prison and when informed of the day of his execution, abandoned himself to a paroxysm of grief.'

The Reverend gentlemen, however, refused to relinquish this lost soul so easily and by the following day, Thomas was reported to be 'more tranquil and appears gradually to be making up his mind to admit his guilt. He now admits, and even solicits, the spiritual consolation he before shunned. Rumours are pretty rife just now, that he not only will confess but may make some important disclosures implicating others'.

At the mercy of the administrating clergy, Thomas eventually succumbed and this announcement appeared in *The Carmarthen Journal* on 4 April, 1845:

It will be satisfactory to the public to know that Thomas Thomas, the wretched man who has been condemned to death for the wilful murder of David Lewis at Trecastle, has at length confessed his guilt.* Not also has he confessed the justice of his sentence but has also acknowledged that he has been guilty of other crimes of a serious character. The execution of this unfortunate but guilty man is definitely fixed to take place in front of the Brecon County Gaol on Thursday next the 10th inst. Preparations for that purpose are already in progress. The final sentence of the law will be carried into effect at 10 o'clock in the forenoon.

* On condition that it was not published until after his death.

The account went on to assure its readers that prisoner Thomas continued to receive a number of religious advisers. The description of him as 'an intelligent and shrewd young man' was borne out by the fact that, hedging his bets, he asked for members of several churches—the Church of England, the Baptists and other Non-Conformists. He was described as being 'resigned to a fate that is fixed and inevitable. He is intent in earnest preparation for the doom that awaits him. His conduct, upon the whole, though decorous, is somewhat capricious and contradictory, indulging, at one period, in the most frantic outbursts of grief, such as a young man must feel with the protracted agony of the gibbet before him.... as if overcome with the desolating reflection, and the utter abandonment of all hope, he wreaks his thoughts upon expression and in all vehement denunciations against the evil companions that first taught him to look familiarly on murder and berates himself and the whole world. The parties in official attendance on him wisely give way while the fit is upon him and wait for the reaction, when gentler and holier thoughts are suggested to him and he evinces the docility of a child.

'He is frequently in the course of the day, found sitting on his wretched pallet, with his hands clasped over his knees, and presenting a picture of sullen and reluctant resignation. With that infirmity of thought peculiar to persons engrossed with one absorbing idea, he often speaks aloud to himself, but only to himself: "To die, to die, so young and such a death!" are phrases frequently in his mouth.

'On Wednesday evening there was a perceptible change in the person and demeanour of Thomas. Though retaining the appearance of vigour, indicated by a powerfully built frame, there was an evident falling away of his flesh; his cheek, which up to that period, retained much of its healthy complexion, assumed occasionally an ashen hue, while the compressed lip, and the sunken and troubled eye, bore testimony to the terrible apprehensions which consumed him.

'On that evening he sat down to dinner and rather mechanically nibbled at a few morsels of food which he seemed to swallow with difficulty. He was observed to sob convulsively and literally water his bread with his tears. As if ashamed of his weakness, he would make an effort to rally and fall again to his meal and make a show of doing something with it. He retired to bed at his usual hour and slept for five hours—'nature's sweet restorer' visited him kindly for the last time and the wretched man lost, in a momentary oblivion, the sense of approaching torture, and the agonising apprehensions that made every thought a scorpion to sting his inmost soul.'

The execution of Thomas Thomas was carried out as planned on 10 April and reported in great detail in *The Carmarthen Journal*:

'At an early hour in the morning crowds of people were pouring throughout every road into the town, and by the appointed hour a concourse estimated at from 15,000 to 20,000 had assembled. Every disposable vehicle was put on requisition to carry people to the scene of suffering. The fashionable phaeton was drawn up side by side with the humble cart, the occupants of each waiting patiently for the hour of execution.'

On the whole the crowd was orderly but 'here and there, however, might be seen a group who forget the propriety of the occasion and in no measured terms, express their satisfaction at the fate that awaited the wretched culprit. This feeling never was very sympathised with and wherever openly avowed was instantly suppressed by the more humane disposition of the multitude.'

The River Tarell separated the assembled crowds and the scaffold, forming 'an admirable barrier' whilst 'numbers of javelin-men,* police and special constables kept the avenues free from all intrusion, but the behaviour of the immense crowd which covered the Merthyr road, the bridge, the trees, and the rising ground beyond was most orderly and decent.'

As for the condemned man, he had risen at four o'clock that dreadful morning and eaten a breakfast of tea and bread and butter. After this he attended a church service with all the other

* Early special security force called upon for important civic functions. They were also used to accompany newly elected MPs when carried into Brecon on a special chair.

prisoners in the prison chapel and took communion. On returning to the condemned cell he was confronted with his personal nemesis, William Calcraft, the Newgate executioner. According to a published report, 'Thomas, on beholding him, shuddered and turned away his eyes. A few commonplace yet kind words from the perfunctory brought him to himself, and he made an effort to reciprocate the affected courtesy of this dreadful minister of the law. A small wicker chair and a piece of stout jack-line hinted to the bewildered convict what he was expected to do.'

Thomas, though passive, was in tears, his eyes closed and his head to one side. He asked the chaplain to give his clothes and his notebook, in which he had copied passages from the scriptures, to his family. He shook hands with all the officers and magistrates present and thanked the prison governor for all he had done for him—then he sat in the chair while Calcraft swiftly pinioned his arms with the rope.

'The wretched convict appeared to take no notice of the spectators, and wept bitterly, holding a handkerchief to his face as well as his pinioned arms would allow him, but his step was wonderfully firm, and at the foot of the steps he turned round to the governor of the gaol and shook hands with him. He then proceeded to where the drop was erected with a faltering step which vainly assumed an air of steadiness and resolution.

'On looking, and it was but for a moment, on the vast and unsympathetic multitude before him, he became dreadfully agitated and closed his eyes as if to shut out the sight. Some slight delay, whether accidental or otherwise,* in the adjustment of the rope, made him turn to the executioner. Here, if at all, it was expected he would make further disclosures that were expected—but he said: "Go on with it and be quick for I have nothing more to say." Just before the trap fell, he was observed to pull the cap lower over his face and then was heard to say, being fluent in Welsh and English, "Arglwydd, maddau i mi" ' (Lord, forgive me)...

---

* There was speculation that Thomas would make a final addition to his confession, implicating others.

'The rope was adjusted round his neck, which was bared by the collar of his shirt being turned down; the bolt was drawn and the wretched man was launched into eternity. A few convulsive shrugs of the shoulders and the contraction of the legs, evidenced his mortal agonies, which, happily, were not much protracted, and the agonising culprit ceased to live about eight minutes after he was turned off..'

After hanging for the statutory hour, to guarantee death, (from strangulation, if nothing else), the body was taken down and examined, before witnesses, by a doctor. A short, mandatory inquest was carried out after which the body was placed in a cheap coffin or box; it was then buried in the prison yard.

On 18 April, 1845, *The Carmarthen Journal* printed the full confession of Thomas Thomas; he described the shooting in this way:

'When we got near Trecastle David Lewis was walking on my left hand and a little before me. I then shot him with my left hand. I held the pistol in my hand for some time opposite his head for I could not get a sight of the end of the barrel. He instantly fell in his double and never groaned, I walked on a few yards then returned to the body. I straightened it else they could not put it in the coffin. I took his money and pocketbook and I put his hat on his face and went away.'

After the killing he had made his way home; 'I hid the mackin-tosh (which he had bought on the day of the murder) in the morning before I got to the village lest people should think me proud. I was busy about home till night. I then went to the village to buy some tobacco. I was taken by the policeman there....'

Upon being asked about his feelings after the shooting, he said, 'My heart was so hard that I thought no more of shooting him than I did of killing a hare. I had no enmity towards David Lewis. If I had not killed him, I should have killed someone else, for I was short of money ... I never was concerned in any other murder but I have been guilty of many other little thefts not worth 3d. I attribute these and all my wicked acts to hearing tales about Dick Turpin and such characters and I thought I could do things quite as well as Dick Turpin. '

A reward of £10 had been offered for the capture and arrest of Thomas Thomas, and David Prosser of The Bridgend Inn, who had informed the authorities of his suspicions, made his claim in due course. He was told, however, that as Superintendent Gwynne had made the actual arrest, *he* was entitled to the reward.

Again, *The Carmarthen Journal* was able to inform its readers of the outcome. Prosser, annoyed at being denied the reward, managed to obtain the murder victim's hat, complete with bullet hole.

'This was soon made public and was the means of gathering some hundreds to Mr Prosser's house, anxious to see the hat in question. The excitement and curiosity continued through the Wednesday before the execution of Thomas. On the second day Mr Prosser had got hold of the extracted ball and this again caused great curiosity. The house was crowded through the two days and very few left without spending at least 6d or 1/-. The liquor sold by Mr Prosser on this occasion yielded him a clear profit of £10 and upwards, and he considered he has received a reward at the hands of Providence.'

VII

Terrible Murder at Weobley

'In the darkness, between ten and eleven o'clock, a poor woman was murdered in a most horrifying manner in a field just outside the antiquated and historic village of Weobley; and the terrible deed has thrown the people of the locality into quite a ferment, the excitement, horror and disgust of the whole district being intensified by the fact that the alleged perpetrators are young men, natives of the village.'

By the time this article appeared in *The Hereford Times* on Saturday, 3 October, 1885, the police had details of the whole sequence of events leading to the dreadful murder of Ann Dickson. The dead woman's friend, forty year old Mary Ann Farrell, had been with her on the night concerned, but had managed to survive a brutal attack by one of the suspected murderers, a man already under arrest.

It transpired that the victim, thirty-three year old Ann Dickson—who also went under the names of Ann Dogerty, Ann Doughety or Ann Cox—had met up with Mary Farrell at Worcester about a month before. They were itinerant workers, referred to in the newspapers as 'tramping women', for the most part living rough and travelling from farm to farm looking for seasonal work. With Mary Farrell's four month old baby and Ann Dickson's five year old daughter, they had walked the 30 odd miles from Worcester to Weobley where they found work picking hops for a Mr Rogers of Homme Farm, Dilwyn. In addition to their wages they were normally given a daily ration of food and a barn to sleep in.

67

On the day of the murder, Wednesday, 30 September, the weather had been so bad, with heavy rain and a high wind, that the hop-pickers had been unable to work in the fields. In addition they were broke and had to borrow a shilling each from the farmer to buy some groceries. Even though it was cold and still pouring with rain, the two women, leaving Ann's little girl in the barn with the other hop-pickers, walked the mile and a half into Weobley—Mary Ann Farrell carrying her baby in her arms, wrapped in a shawl. When they reached the village they bought some bread and meat from a small grocer's shop near the Red Lion. Ann Dickson said she was expecting her common-law husband, Daniel Cox, to meet her that evening. He had just been released from Worcester Gaol after serving three weeks imprisonment for beating her up whilst drunk. Despite this, the previous Saturday she had sent him two shillings and twopence for the train fare from Worcester and was expecting him that evening.

Having purchased the food the two women went to the tap-room of The Red Lion while they waited for Daniel's arrival—it was now about half-past six in the evening. They were soon joined by two fellow hop-pickers, Mark Hill and a man called 'Blackbird', and as the drink flowed there was 'much merriment and laughter'. Ann Dickson was described as a lively soul with a 'very cheery and pleasant manner' and fortified by the encouragement and free drinks afforded by the others, she was soon singing loudly.

A little later that evening two local men, who had been drinking steadily all afternoon, decided to join the party of hop-pickers—John Hill, known as 'Sailor Jack' and John Williams known as 'Irish Jack'. Both men were in their early thirties and very similar in looks and build—they were both strong, sinewy and mean. Sailor Jack, as his name would imply, had travelled the world on board ship and was known locally as a tough and unpredictable character, prone to bouts of drunken violence. Irish Jack was a painter and glazier who lived in Weobley with his elderly mother; he, too, tended to become aggressive when drunk and as a result had twice been gaoled for violent affray.

Both men were well-known in the area as a pair of bullies yet, by all accounts, there was nothing churlish about their behaviour

as they drank and chatted with the two women that evening—
they bought drinks, joined in the singing and even played with
Mary Farrell's baby. The atmosphere was boisterous but good
natured. Williams was carrying his favourite stick, which was a
vicious looking object made of ash with a large knob on the end,
the size of a man's fist. He was playfully brandishing the stick in
the air during the evening's revelry until Mary Farrell took it
from him, half-jokingly, afraid he might hit the baby by mistake.
She later gave it back and continued with her friendly banter until
she went to sit by the fire, where Williams followed her. While he
was playing with the child he put his hand on her knee and
'pinched it in a familiar way'. She took offence at this, and 'gave
him a black look and went and sat on the other side of the fire.'
But, she later told the police, when he followed her she 'put a
round table between to prevent him interfering with me. But he
removed the table and came for me again'. After this she said she
'took herself off to another corner of the kitchen and avoided
him.'

At about half-past eight, Sailor Jack, who had been 'chum-
ming' with Ann Dickson all evening, left the pub and went back

Weobley, with The Red Lion in front of the church tower

to his lodgings to change his clothes. When he returned to the inn he was wearing his Sunday best—a dark coloured suit. More drinks were consumed and the singing and laughter continued until the women left the pub about nine-thirty. The weather, by this time, had worsened; it was raining heavily and there was a strong wind. It was also very dark as the moon was completely hidden by cloud. As Daniel Cox had failed to appear, the two women expressed a fear of walking back to the farm alone. Sailor Jack Hill immediately offered to accompany them, saying that he was going to Homme Farm anyway. Mary Farrell said later that she trusted Hill because he was a salt-bird, or sailor, like her husband and son.

So it was that the women accepted his offer and left the pub 'chatting merrily' between themselves. They noticed Williams standing in the doorway, talking to some friends. Seeing the lethal looking stick in his hands, Mary Farrell, clutching her baby, said she was frightened of him and suggested they go to the police station and ask for protection.

But Ann Dickson, made merry and carefree from the night's drinking, merely laughed at her and said she was being 'soft'. Still uneasy, Mary followed her friend and Hill down the road past the church and towards the pitch blackness of the open fields. The two women walked ahead as they crossed the first field, chattering 'about their own affairs' as they went. But Hill kept trying to butt in, at first trying to tell them about his sea-faring adventures and then, making 'some vulgar suggestions', which the women ignored. At one point, Mary Farrell, annoyed at his persistence, snapped: 'Mind your own business—I'll talk to you in a minute, young man!'

After walking for about half a mile, they came to a ploughed field; Mary Ann went first to open the gate and was immediately attacked from the front—she saw the flash of a stick and then felt a violent blow to her head, which badly damaged her right eye. The assault was so sudden and the night was so dark that she failed to see her assailant. She fell to the ground, her baby still in her arms, and remained dazed for a few seconds. When she came to, Williams, whom she suspected had attacked her with his stick, was attempting to rape her. In the fierce struggle that ensued she twice managed to get to her feet only to be thrown to the ground once more. Enraged by her resistance, he snatched the baby from her and flung it into the grass some five yards away, where it lay screaming with fright.

At this point, Mary Farrell, desperate to save herself and her child—for her attacker had threatened to kill her if she didn't submit to the rape—had no idea what had happened to Ann Dickson or Hill. After begging for mercy to no avail, Mary, with commendable presence of mind, decided on a cunning strategy. She suggested to Williams that they walk a little further to the barn where she was sleeping and, where, she promised, he could spend the whole night with her. Luckily, Williams agreed and the two set off across the field—as Mary carried her baby in her right arm, the blood was streaming from her cut eye and soaking into the shawl. Concealing her pain and fear she tried to make light of her injuries by chatting flirtatiously with her attacker, even allowing him to walk with his arm around her waist.

As soon as they reached the shepherd's cottage, Mary Ann broke away from him, rushed up to the door and screamed 'MURDER!' At this, her assailant ran off and the shepherd, seeing her injuries, took her across to the hop-pickers' barn. She was bruised and badly shaken by what had happened. Her petti-coats were torn and filthy and all her teeth had been loosened with one knocked out completely. Not surprisingly, she spent a restless night, unable to sleep, wondering what had happened to Ann Dickson. When, by daybreak, her friend had still not returned, Mary Ann knew she must be dead.

As indeed she was. Between six and seven the following morning, two roadmen, William Jones and Richard Preece, were on their way to work when they came across the body of Ann Dickson, 'lying up against an oak tree, about half a mile from the village', near the gate where Mary Ann Farrell had been attacked. Her arms were half-raised to her head, the fists clenched and the poor woman's face had been 'smashed to pieces'—so much so that one of her eyes was gone completely and the remaining features were unrecognisable. Ann Dickson's skirt, torn and muddied, was pulled up about her thighs and her stockings hung about her ankles. The grass surrounding the body was thick with blood and there were signs that she had been dragged some distance. Not far from the body they found an ash stick, split in two, and a little further along, the heavy end which had broken off completely.

While one of the men stayed with the body, the other ran into Weobley to tell the police. By this time, however, Mary Farrell, seeing that Ann Dickson had not returned, had already walked back into the village as soon as it was light and told Superintendent Ovens what had happened the night before. Mary could barely stand and her face was in a terrible mess; her right eye was black and so swollen it had closed completely and she had a number of vicious scratches on her cheeks. On hearing her account the policeman ran straight round to the cottage where John Williams lived with his elderly mother. John was still in bed and his clothes, scattered about the bedroom, were heavily stained with blood. When awakened, and arrested on suspicion of murder, Williams 'expressed great surprise' and denied killing Ann Dickson, saying that he had been with 'the other woman but knew who struck the blow that killed her'.

As soon as John Williams was under lock and key the police headed for Hill's lodgings, only to be told that he had run away. Assuming that, as a sailor, he would try to skip the country on board ship, the police sent urgent messages by telegraph to Newport, Cardiff and Swansea, offering this description of the wanted man:

John Hill
A Seaman, Native of Weobley.
(But has only recently returned from Sea)
32 or 33 years of age, 5ft.6in high, dark hair
small, light moustache, no beard or whiskers,
has a ship tattooed on right arm, nose slightly
turned to the side, dressed in dark or black
cloth coat, vest and trousers, soft billy cock
hat turned up at sides and dented in the top,
clean cotton shirt with light brown stripes,
and elastic sided boots.

By the Friday evening, two days after the murder and about the same time as the inquest was under way, Hill was arrested at Newport. Using a false name, he had actually gone to the local police station to ask for a ticket entitling him to a night's lodging at the workhouse. Realising who he was, an officer pushed back the right sleeve of his coat and 'laid bare the full-rigged ship tattoo on his arm'. He had scratches on his face and his clothes were blood-stained—and when the police accused him of being the runaway sailor wanted for the murder at Weobley, Hill 'trembled like an aspen leaf and shed tears'.

John Williams was immediately taken into custody and the following day, Saturday, 3 October, transferred to Hereford by train, handcuffed at the wrist to Ovens. Crowds had already gathered at the station to see him arrive; a reporter described him as 'looking very dejected; a man of medium height and attired in an over-large suit of clothes, and a billy-cock hat. There was little in his personal appearance to distinguish him from the ordinary labouring man—his large, crooked nose was the most prominent feature..... As the crowd pressed forward to obtain a glance at him a discomposed tremor passed and repassed over his countenance, and he moved his small, sharp eyes about restlessly, as if unable to confront the indignant gaze of the people around.' He was immediately taken to Hereford Gaol and remanded in custody on suspicion of murder.

On the evening of his arrest, Friday, 2 October, the inquest on Ann Dickson had opened at the Boardroom of the Workhouse in Weobley, before the coroner, Mr H. Moore. The woman's mutilated body had been taken to the Workhouse where a postmortem examination was made by Dr William Walker. He established that her death was caused by a vicious attack with a blunt instrument—in his opinion this *could* have been the ash stick belonging to John Williams—the blows being so violent that the bones of the face had penetrated the brain. Her features had been completely obliterated and her common-law husband, Daniel Cox, newly arrived from Worcester, only managed to identify her by the fact that part of her left breast was missing—he confirmed that Ann Dickson had it surgically removed some years before.

Despite this harrowing evidence, Williams, who was present during the proceedings, 'maintained an exceedingly indifferent demeanour throughout'. He appeared wearing 'a dirty pair of trousers and an equally dirty slop'. He was, according to one witness, 'a short, muscular fellow, with a high cheek bone and sunken eyes, his features being angular in outline, but to the casual observer there is nothing rough or brutal about his appearance. On the contrary he presents a rather contemplative countenance, with a vein of humour lurking about his mouth and eyes'.

One of the first witnesses to be called was Mary Ann Farrell, described as 'a poorly-clad, gypsy looking woman'. Still bearing the marks of her attack, and clutching her baby in her arms, she confirmed that the body she had seen in the Workhouse morgue was that of Ann Dickson. She had first met her, she said, in the Tramp Ward at Worcester Workhouse in August and they had become friends. While she was giving evidence, Williams looked on with 'a melancholy air'. After she had given a graphic account of the night of the murder, the two roadmen who found the body were called.

When Daniel Cox, described as 'a ragged looking tramping fellow' was called to the witness-box he said he had lived with Ann Dickson for more than four years. He was clearly affected by her death and cried the whole time he was giving evidence. At this point it was decided to adjourn the enquiry until the arrival of the other prisoner, Hill, from Newport.

On the Sunday after the murder, scores of people tramped across the fields to make a 'morbid inspection' of the scene, which, after so much rain, reduced the area to a muddy quagmire—some even came over from Leominster, simply to stare at the blood stained grass or gather outside the shepherd's cottage, hoping to catch sight of Mary Ann Farrell or Ann Dickson's little girl, to whom they gave coppers. In the evening the vicar of Weobley, Rev J.S. Crook, preached a sermon which, according to the regular congregation, was 'the most earnest and eloquent' for a long time. He spoke of hell-fire and warned his flock in thunderous terms about the danger of strong drink and 'frequenting public houses, drinking and quarrelling, and carrying on ribaldrous behaviour'. He urged his parishioners to renounce intoxicating drink in favour of Bible reading and to frequent, not bawdy ale-houses, but places of worship. Preachers for miles around took to their pulpits with renewed vigour, for temperance was always a favourite theme with Victorian clerics and the murder in their midst provided them with a perfect example of strong drink leading to acts of the utmost depravity.

Ann Dickson's funeral was held shortly after nine o'clock the following day, Monday, 5 October. To 'avoid morbid curiosity' the police had brought the time forward from ten-thirty so only Daniel Cox, Ann's little girl and a few villagers were present. It was a pathetic affair—a real pauper's burial. The deal coffin was taken to Weobley churchyard in the Workhouse hearse, followed by Daniel Cox and the young girl. The inscription on the lid was brief: AD, the initials of the dead woman and 33, her age when she died. Daniel Cox seemed overwhelmed with grief as he led the little girl by the hand; they were both dressed in 'rags and tatters' and despite the vicar's efforts to console them, continued to weep bitterly.

Whilst appearing as the principal witness during the inquest, Mary Ann Farrell and her baby were given lodgings at the police station. Accustomed to rough work, a poor diet and only straw to sleep on, she flourished under the comparative luxury of the police quarters and gradually recovered from her attack, though the sight in her right eye was still impaired.

As for Ann Dickson's little girl—her name was never disclosed—no sooner was the child's mother buried than some of the hop-picking women started fighting over who should take care of her. Sadly, these brawls did not stem from compassion but from avarice—the girl was described as 'a remarkably smart, precocious child, with dark hair and expressive eyes'—one that would clearly make an appealing attraction for begging purposes. When Daniel Cox heard about the fights he argued that he, if anyone, should take care of the child; the police agreed and arranged for them both to lodge with a Mrs Davies, who, much taken with the child, dressed her 'in neat mourning clothes at her own expense'.

On Friday, 9 October, both Hill and Williams were brought before the magistrates in the Governor's room at Hereford Gaol and formally charged with the murder of Ann Dickson. Dressed in 'grim prison garb' the similarity between the two men was remarkable and, it was noted, 'they might have been brought up to answer a charge of having been drunk and disorderly for all the concern their countenances betrayed. Serious they certainly looked, yet they were withal composed and self-possessed and hardly appeared to realise the awful gravity of their position.' So similar were the two men that a reporter felt sure that, without 'the distinctive numeral badges they wore' it would have been impossible to 'distinguish the Irishman and the Sailor'.

During the short proceedings, Williams proclaimed to be partially deaf and said he had heard little of what was said. Despite his disability he elected to defend himself when he and Hill were formally charged and the committal proceedings were set for the following Monday in Weobley.

On the Monday morning there were large crowds of people from as far as Leominster waiting outside the 'spacious and light-some new court-house', anxious to catch a glimpse of the accused men. Shortly before eleven o'clock the handcuffed prisoners arrived from Hereford Gaol in an omnibus. They had a rough reception—people in the crowd 'hooted and hissed excitedly' as they were hurried into the building. When they reached the cells Williams 'flung himself against the wall' in a faint. Both men looked haggard; Williams was an especially sorry sight for he had lost a lot of weight and was shabbily dressed.

After the charges were read out, Mr Corner, for the prosecution, gave an emotive summary of the case. According to a reporter from *The Hereford Times* 'both prisoners stood up straight in the dock, with their hands hanging at their sides— Williams looking thoughtful and earnest and Hill was wearing an anxious expression'. When Corner described the actual killing of Ann Dickson, he spoke with such expression that Williams 'was visibly moved, his features twitched uneasily, and he turned very pale. Hill also soon afterwards lost his colour and evidently felt the force of the evidence.' In fact, the prosecutor spoke in such a 'masterly manner' and was 'so forcible and eloquent' that by the time he had finished many in the court were in tears—including the police.

When Corner had finished his summary of the case he urged the magistrates to commit the two men for trial for murder and, in addition, further charge Williams with inflicting grievous bodily harm to Mary Ann Farrell. Exhausted by his efforts it was left to his son, Arthur Corner, to question the witnesses. Once more, Mrs Farrell was required to recall the terrible events that night. When Williams, who was defending himself, was asked if he wished to question Farrell, he shouted at her and accused her of lying. But the woman stood her ground and refused to be intimidated.

When questioned at length, Dr Walker, who had carried out the postmortem on Ann Dickson's body, told the court that the victim had put up a tremendous fight, inflicting deep scratches on Hill's face and body. He had even found particles of human skin under her finger nails.*

After hearing all the evidence the two men were charged and cautioned—John Hill made no comment whatsoever but John Williams, after hotly denying that he had anything to do with the killing, began a rambling account of the night of the murder. Mr Corner, very fairly, warned him not to proceed in case, in the absence of anyone guarding his interests, he might incriminate himself. A Catholic priest, Father Henry Benedict Mackey, talked quietly to him in the dock and advised him to say nothing. The Bench then ordered that both men stand trial on a charge of the 'Wilful Murder' of Ann Dickson and, in the case of John Williams, the additional charge of 'grievous bodily harm against Mary Ann Farrell'. The case would be heard at the next Gloucester Assizes, on 7 November, 1885.

The Coroner, on resuming his inquest, expressed his annoyance that, disregarding usual practice, the magistrates had reached their verdict before the Coroner's jury. Besides printing coverage of both enquiries on Saturday, 17 October, *The Hereford Times*

* Since the discovery of DNA, identification of the murderer in this case would be a relatively simple operation matching the two tissue types.

also reported the fact that Ann Dickson's little girl, 'a very bright and interesting child' had been 'taken from the man Cox, by the police, with the hope of bettering her prospects socially and morally.' She was placed in the Hereford Workhouse and the police were hoping to 'obtain the patronage of some influential persons on her behalf'. Mary Ann Farrell and her baby were also allowed to stay, temporarily, at least, in the Workhouse.*

Three letters also appeared in the same edition. One, from an irate inhabitant of Weobley, expressed disgust that Williams had received 'moral and monetary support' from Father Benedict Mackey and 'a Papist magistrate'. It even went so far as to suggest that the two gentlemen were partly to blame for Williams's present predicament, having previously paid his court fines for him.

Another letter disputed Father Mackey's view, expressed in the same newspaper, that strong drink was responsible for the tragedy; it was, in the writer's opinion, merely an excuse for it. John Bradford, a Herefordian, wrote deploring the wretched pauper's burial given to Ann Dickson. He referred to her as a 'poor, misguided and ill-starred' woman who was 'foully murdered by lustful brutes'. And, he pointed out, she had 'died in defence of her honour, such as it was; if she lived with Cox as she did, she was as much married to him as she would have been if she had paid a few shillings at the registrar's office to make the concubinage legal. Humbug is humbug.' Finally, he asked: 'Was it not a pity that there were not enough kind hearts in Weobley to see that the name of the ill-fated woman was put upon her coffin in full and not in initials?'

The trial of John Hill and John Williams was held on Monday, 7 November, at Gloucester, before Mr Justice Field. Mr Charles Darling* and the Hon A. Lyttleton, were acting as prosecuting counsel; the judge had ordered a Mr Ram to defend John Hill and a Mr Griffiths had been secured on John Williams's behalf.

* The little girl was eventually placed in a 'respectable home'.
* Later Sir Charles Darling, KC. High Court Judge who presided over the trial of Major Herbert Rowse Armstrong at Hereford Assizes in 1922.

Mary Ann Farrell

John Hill   John Williams

The case occasioned such interest that the newspapers dedi-
cated countless pages describing the whole affair for their
readers. An hour before the court opened 'the surging crowd
struggled and almost fought their way to the entrance doors, only
to be turned back by the police on the account of the court being
filled. One division of the gallery was solely set apart for females;
the judge having the previous day ordered that women were not
to be kept out because the evidence in the case happened to be of

an obscene nature. 'If they chose to hear disgusting details which came out in the administration of justice, they might do so.'

As the judge entered the court it was noted that he was carrying the 'black cap'—a square of black silk which was traditionally placed upon the head of the judge whilst pronouncing the death sentence—which he laid on the bench as he sat down. When the two prisoners were brought up from the cells and stood before him in the dock 'every eye was fixed upon them'. Williams wore the same dirty slop jacket and old trousers that he appeared in at both the inquest and the magistrates' court. Their similarity was again remarked upon although Hill was said to have a more 'dare-devil look about him'. Both prisoners looked haggard and careworn, especially Williams, who 'looked straight in front the whole day of the trial, scarcely moving his head, hands or feet at all; but Hill twisted his head and eyes constantly, as though he could not help surveying the people, the court generally, and the scene as a whole, with unfeigned curiosity. They listened earnestly to all that was said, but did not at all evince any marked signs of uneasiness, except that once or twice Hill, during Mr Darling's recital of the more terrible details, nervously twitched his fingers.'

Yet, when the judge had to have explained to him the meaning of one or two colloquialisms which he failed to understand, Hill seemed 'quite amused' and smiled broadly when the judge later made some exasperated comment to one of the barristers. Williams, on the other hand, 'kept his head on one side and looked deeply concerned; he is rather deaf so it is doubtful whether he heard anybody's speech distinctly throughout the trial, except that of his counsel, Mr Griffiths, whose stentorian voice at times made all the echoes of the old court-house ring.'

His religious adviser, Father Mackey, remained close to Williams throughout the trial; it was he who had managed to raise sufficient funds to secure the services of Griffiths to defend Williams and had attended both the inquest and the magistrates' hearing to offer him every support.

Early on in the proceedings the judge had 'ordered chairs to be brought for the prisoners, and Williams, who had been holding firmly on to the front rail of the dock, at once availed himself of a seat. Hill, however, remained standing till Superintendent Ovens was being examined, and then, he also sat down, as though he was getting really tired of being on his legs so long.'

'Towards five o'clock, Mr Darling rose to sum up the whole case for the prosecution, and his second speech, like his first, was a model of perspicuity'. After this, Mr Ram, rose to defend John Hill 'with silvery tongue'. He rightly contended that he was faced with a near impossible task when dealing with the public prejudice that existed against both prisoners. Having heard all the gruesome details of Ann Dickson's murder, feelings were high against his client in particular—he had, he admitted, evidently sustained a number of scratches during a struggle that night, his clothing was heavily bloodstained and he had attempted to escape by jumping ship. Despite this, Mr Ram suggested that if, as the prosecution proclaimed, Ann Dickson was beaten to death with a stick such as the one that belonged to Williams—found broken at the scene of the crime—surely this must point the finger at Williams, not Hill. His client, he went on, had no such stick, and if he had used it that night then Williams must have given it to him. Having said this, Mr Ram sat down 'with the air of a brave man who had done his best'.

It was now the turn of Mr Griffiths, defending Williams: he pointed out that much had been made by the prosecution of Williams's alleged attack on Mary Farrell. This, he reminded the jurors, was not the crime for which his client was on trial. There was no direct evidence, he insisted, to prove that Williams had attacked and killed Ann Dickson. He also drew their attention to the fact that when arrested Williams had not denied he had been with Mary Farrell that night. But he *had* denied striking Ann Dickson but said he knew who had struck the blow that killed her? Who else could he mean but John Hill? It was true, he conceded, that his client was at The Red Lion that night and that he was carrying his stick but, unlike Hill, he did not attempt to run away after the murder—he was found in his bed next day. John Hill, not John Williams, he urged the jury, was the murderer of Ann Dickson.

That concluded both speeches for the defence; despite their efforts one court reporter commented that even 'before the judge commenced his summing up it was clear that the case for the prosecution had not been at all shaken, and there was little hope for either prisoner.'

The judge's closing speech was equally devastating. According to *The Hereford Times* reporter 'from the beginning to the end of his speech he never uttered a word which might tell in their favour—as, indeed, he could not. When he had finished the jury instantly began to consult together. They were asked if they wished to retire and the foreman replied that he thought not. They had all evidently made up their minds and it seemed to only remain for the foreman to make sure that they were unanimous before he gave the fatal "verdict of them all". The consideration of the matter did not occupy them more than three minutes and then, in a clear voice, but with a flush upon his face, uttered the word "guilty" in regard to each. Everybody seemed to feel that it was a crushing dreadful moment for the prisoners, but they did not evince the least emotion'.

The judge assured the jury that he fully concurred with their verdict, indeed emphasising that, in his opinion, it would be impossible to come to any other conclusion but that both men were guilty as charged. He then 'assumed the black cap and the silence of death prevailed.' He told them that he had now but one duty to perform, and that was to pass sentence of death upon each of them. This he did so in those chilly, formal words always used upon such occasions. Hill and Williams 'fixedly gazed at the judge as he read the sentence of death, as though they scarcely seemed able to realise the horrible import of the words—"There to be hanged by the neck till you are dead".'

Having issued the terrible sentence, the judge added: '...but I am permitted to add a prayer, which I do submit in all sincerity; and it is that the Lord may have mercy on your souls'.

The two prisoners showed no outward display of emotion as they left the dock but as they reached the steps leading to the cells, Williams fainted and had to be carried the rest of the way by two warders. Soon after both prisoners were sent by train to

Hereford County Gaol to await execution. They had been driven to Gloucester Railway Station in a cab, handcuffed to two warders, where quite a crowd, 'principally of the rough element' had gathered. As Hill and Williams arrived, 'the crowd hooted and made a rush for them'. Williams, especially, found this unnerving and 'got terribly frightened'. As the train drew near to Hereford he became agitated but the warders managed to convey them to the prison without further ugly scenes.

The date for the execution of John Hill and John Williams was set for Monday, 23 November, 1885. There was a concerted effort, orchestrated by Father Benedict Mackey, to obtain a reprieve for John Williams; but it was the general consensus that, of the two, Williams was the more reprehensible character. The appeal was duly rejected by the Home Office and the execution scheduled to go ahead as planned. Since the trial they had been kept in separate cells, constantly watched by teams of warders. Given access to books of a religious nature, Hill read avidly but Williams, 'being able to read but imperfectly' did not.

During this time the vicar of Weobley managed to extract a full confession from John Hill which was printed in *The Hereford Times* on 21 November. In it, Sailor Jack admitted that Mary Ann Farrell had spoken the truth about the night of the murder. After she had been attacked by Williams, Ann Dickson had screamed and tried to run for the police. But Hill had stopped her and tried to rape her—she struggled valiantly and was still fighting when Williams ran back from the shepherd's cottage after Farrell had called 'MURDER!' Williams, seeing that the woman was gripping Hill's finger with her teeth, intervened by dealing her a vicious blow with his stick. Hill maintained that he got to his feet, retrieved his hat and left Williams and the woman together and swore that he didn't strike her once, either with his fist or a stick.

While awaiting execution John Hill wrote a number of letters to his family. In these, and during their visits, he vehemently denied being guilty of murder, only, he said, of assault; he also urged his brothers to avoid the demon drink. On the family's last visit, on 18 November, Hill's elderly mother 'seemed completely broken down with grief'. 'The poor old soul,' said a reporter, 'has got to look much older and more feeble since the inquest at Weobley and in her sudden decrepitude she leans heavily on her stick. Considerable sympathy is felt for her at Weobley for she has been an honest, hard-working old woman all her life.... The other sons, like their mother, were of industrious habits, and they all feel acutely the sad position of their brother and the degradation which they imagine he has brought upon them.' Hill was allowed one final visit, with his brother James, the following Saturday, after which it was said he became 'very moody and quiet'.

John Williams's widowed mother and one of her sons came from Weobley to see him for the last time. On Saturday they were accompanied by Father Mackey—all three were crying copiously. They had to talk to Williams through two iron grids with a space between, in which stood the prison Governor. After some crying and sobbing on both sides, the mother asked: 'How do you feel, my poor boy?' He replied, between sobs, that he was pretty well in health, but it was observable to them, dusky and gloomy as the corridor was, that he looked paler. His brother Richard asked if he was very low, and he answered, 'No'. Asked whether he had a comfortable bed, he said 'middling'. Had he pretty good food? 'Yes, pretty fair,' was the reply. He told them that they had been given 'steaks and chops and a liberal quantity of milk to drink'. He begged his mother not to 'vex about him as he hoped to meet her in heaven'.

Williams did his best to comfort his mother by saying he was quite happy. He begged her forgiveness for what he had done, to which she replied: 'My dear, you have done nothing against me, except that I wanted you to keep from bad company; that is all, my dear. I freely forgive you, and God will forgive you, I am sure, for I have given you up to Almighty God.'

At the end of the twenty minute interview Williams's mother begged to be allowed to kiss her son through the bars—her request was granted but she became even more distressed and had to be carried away to the prison entrance, 'crying bitterly'.

The Hereford Times stated that up until the night before his execution, Hill slept soundly and ate well. 'Williams, however' it went on, 'was very restless on Saturday and Sunday nights, being terribly anxious about his spiritual welfare, continually going on his knees praying to the Almighty for mercy.' Both men, it was said, no doubt guided by their religious mentors, blamed their downfall on drink. Williams had once taken the pledge and remained sober for eight months, during which time he earned good money as a painter. Described as 'not a badly disposed fellow' when sober but when intoxicated he was 'easily excited and when exasperated, not so easily appeased'.

As Williams's grieving mother was seeing her errant son for the last time, the public hangman, James Berry, was on his way from Bradford for the execution. It was an apt choice in some respects, for he wholeheartedly supported the temperance movement and was, himself, a recent convert to abstinence; he was to say later that, apart from juveniles, he had never hanged a teetotaller. At the time Berry had only been a public executioner for a year—and at thirty-six was the youngest on the Home Office payroll. Yet, within that year he had already hanged thirty-five persons, and by the end of his career, seven years later, he had hanged more than two hundred men and women.

Berry arrived in Hereford a day early as the law only required him to attend the prison on the day before an execution. His early arrival allowed him plenty of time to make all the arrangements and acquaint himself with the historic cathedral city of Hereford. His assistant would measure and weigh the condemned men to enable him to determine the best drop for an instantaneous death, using a Table of Drops which he had devised. Contrary to prison procedure, however, on the Sunday, instead of inspecting the condemned men incognito, he actually entered their cells and introduced himself as the man who would 'launch them into eternity'.

Recalling the meeting he said later: 'The first I saw was Hill, who was undoubtedly the worst of the two. He was an evil fellow, with a hang-dog look and a bulging brow, and when I entered the cell he assumed an air of bravado.'

Taken aback by his attitude, Berry warned: 'Wait until morning when you stand on the edge of doom with the rope round your neck. We'll see if you laugh then!'

Still smiling defiantly, Hill asked him what 'sort of drop' he would give him—in other words, would he suffer. 'The cool way in which he asked me the question surprised and angered me,' went on Berry, already accustomed to command terror by his presence. 'Here was a man on the verge of death, who ought to have been preparing to meet his Maker, pretending to take an interest in the arrangements of the hangman.'

According to Berry, more laughter followed during this bizarre interview and Hill even cracked jokes about his body weight—10st 10lbs—speculating on the pull it would have on the rope. Poignantly, however, at some point in their exchange, Hill's bravado slipped and he asked: 'Will it hurt?'

'His question told me something,' recalled the hangman, triumphantly. 'Like all the rest of the bullies, he had a weak spot—the terror of physical pain.'

His answer to Hill's question was without mercy: 'You will get the same death as all the other people I hang. I do not intend to make any difference in your case and you can take my word that you will die instantaneously, though you do not deserve so easy a fate.'

Meanwhile *The Hereford Times* reported that 'in every dissenting chapel in the city, and also in the parish church and in the chapels at Weobley, earnest prayers for the reconciliation of the two men with their God, before it was too late, were offered up.' Indeed, in churches throughout the county of Herefordshire, sermons were preached on the two prisoners' downfall and the terrible punishment they must suffer the following day. Local missionary and temperance groups took to the streets and held services in which the part played by alcohol in the dreadful murder was the central theme. One such rally was held opposite the Kerry Arms, on the Sunday evening, no doubt hoping to catch the drinkers as they staggered home at closing time. Berry attended this meeting and was seen to be listening attentively.

The execution of Hill and Williams was set for eight o'clock on the Monday morning; the weather turned out to be foggy and depressingly overcast. It was to be the first execution carried out within the precincts of the prison since the abolition of public hangings in 1868. The last public spectacle at Hereford was the execution of Thomas Watkins, four years earlier, amid 'disgraceful scenes of levity and rowdyism'. By way of contrast, the small crowd 'of the lower classes' that had gathered in nearby Workhouse Lane and Commercial Road that morning, were quite subdued. They waited patiently, as the bell from a nearby church began to toll; a few people gathered in shop-doorways, watching for the raising of the black flag above the prison, which would signal that the two men were dead. Some, however, showed their distaste for the whole procedure by drawing down their window blinds. One man, the licensee of a public house in the Commercial Road, refused to serve anyone until the execution was over, as he said he didn't want 'to make a penny' from the dreadful affair.

Inside, John Williams was praying fervently, surrounded by his spiritual advisors. Hill was also supported by several clerics but approached his end more stoically. Once pinioned by Berry in their cells, they walked to the scaffold, which in this case was some distance. Ideally, to avoid the prolonged torment and, of course, the opportunity to make a last minute fight for life, this was usually kept to a few yards. The scaffold had been especially constructed by a local carpenter and over the weekend Berry and his assistant had tested the whole apparatus, using appropriate weights. On the way to the scaffold Williams, 'his face livid with fright' had to be assisted by two warders and continually cried: 'Jesus, have mercy on me!' A priest walked beside him, reciting the Catholic burial service for the dead. Father Mackey, having supported Williams throughout his ordeal, was too distraught to witness the execution.

Hill, on the other hand, needed no assistance from the warders and remained silent; he did not even join in the prayers as the chaplain read the Church of England burial service. According to Berry, in a subsequent interview in *The Hereford Times*, on reaching the scaffold Hill stepped onto it 'firm as a rock'. He later referred to him as 'a lion of a man' who had said he preferred to die rather than spend the rest of his life in prison.

Outside the prison, at two minutes past eight, 'the drop was distinctly heard, falling with a heavy thud, and in a few seconds more the black flag was hoisted over the new portion of the high wall of the prison, facing Commercial Road, below the gaol entrance.' People gathered in the road then began to drift away. 'A good many, however, lingered in scattered knots, hoping to see some of those who had played a part in carrying out the extreme penalty of the law, leaving the gaol.'

After twenty minutes or so a number of people grew tired of waiting and walked away. Others stayed to see the official notice confirming the execution nailed to the door of the prison, before joining the large crowd that had already gathered at Barrs Court railway station. As Berry boarded the 9.35 a.m. train to Bradford, the people surged forwards to catch a glimpse of him but, according to an eye-witness, there was 'no manifestation of feeling for or against him'.

The requisite Coroner's inquest into the death of Hill and Williams began at eleven o'clock that morning. The jury were told that, soon after the execution, the prison doctor had climbed down a ladder to inspect the bodies and pronounced them dead. Death in both cases was caused by the dislocation of the neck and would have been instantaneous. A few moments after he had pulled the lever Berry had peered into the hole and noted with satisfaction that both bodies were still and 'hung like leaden weights on the end of the ropes'. It was, he told the witnesses, 'the most perfect execution he had ever seen'.

VIII

A Family Affair

Although the case of Major Herbert Rowse Armstrong has become one of the cause célèbres of the twentieth century he was not the only solicitor to be charged with killing his wife.

An earlier, equally interesting but less well-known case, was that of another solicitor, Edmund Edmonds, of Newent, in Gloucestershire; he was also charged, in 1872, with killing his wife, not with poison but with a violent blow to the head. At the time they died, the wives of both solicitors were in their late forties, and, according to the husbands accused of killing them, suffering from illnesses associated with the menopause. Mrs Edmonds's death occurred in 1867 and, as no crime was suspected, her death certificate was duly signed by the local doctor, Matthew Bass-Smith, a chief protagonist in the subsequent drama. The cause of death was given as apoplexy and no questions were asked.

Five years later, the widower Edmonds was still living in Newent, his household consisting of his two younger sons, Ralph and Oscar, (an elder boy, Edmund, had emigrated to Australia soon after his mother's death), his twenty-two year old niece, Jeannette, and his forty year old sister-in-law, Mary Matthews, known as Aunt Polly. Jeannette, who was to feature so dramatically in this story, had been one of seven children made fatherless by the early death of Edmonds's brother in 1859. Having no daughter of their own, Edmonds and his late wife had taken her into their family where she developed into an attractive, well-educated, and self-assertive young woman. Unfortunately, she was entirely dependent on her uncle and was obliged to remedy this by working as a secretary in his legal practice. The business was run from a room on the ground floor of the family home which had been converted into an office.

The terms of her employment are not known—whether, for instance, she received a salary or was simply working in exchange for her keep. What becomes perfectly clear as the story unfolds is that Jeannette was either an extremely devious young woman or she was allowed an extraordinary degree of freedom within the household. It was later revealed that, somehow or other, whether through sheer cunning on her part or lack of vigilance on that of her guardians, she had managed to conduct a passionate love affair with one of her uncle's associates.

The relationship had been flourishing for a period of four years and Edmonds only discovered it by chance one day in the office. While Jeannette was out of the room Edmonds decided to take a look at a letter he had seen her writing. He professed to be shocked to see that it was addressed to a man called Anthony and was of an intimate nature. Certain phrases that caught his eye— referring to the design and intricacies of her underwear—left no doubt in his mind as to the nature of the relationship between the recipient and his young ward. In true Victorian fashion he confronted Jeannette on her return, saying: 'You hussy, I've found you out.'

It may have been the ridiculous pomposity of this remark or the hypocrisy of it coming from the lips of her uncle, a man with a reputation as a womaniser, that made the young woman give him a 'saucy' look and laugh outright. Outraged, her uncle slapped her face. Even this did not intimidate her and throughout the fearful remonstrations that followed she absolutely refused to divulge her admirer's proper name. Unknown to Edmonds, Jeannette's lover for the past four years had been Dr Matthew Bass-Smith, formerly the local doctor, but now retired to London. He was a man well into his fifties, with a wife and four children. (A fifth was yet to be born). Perhaps in an attempt to glorify what was, in fact, a rather sordid and clandestine attachment the lovers had adopted the names Anthony and Cleopatra.

According to Edmonds's version of events he was so infuriated by his niece's recalcitrance that he showed her the door, though she later insisted that she left the house on account of a quarrel over a clerical mistake. Either way, she determined to leave and the next morning borrowed 37 shillings from her cousin, Ralph, so that she could go to to Newport to see her mother. From there she wrote to Matthew Bass-Smith and asked him to go to her uncle's house in Newent and fetch all her belongings. Edmonds was enraged when he opened the door to find the doctor on his doorstep, demanding his young mistress's boxes. He shook his fist and became 'very excited' when he realised that Jeannette's secret lover was none other than Bass-Smith, for he and the doctor had already fallen out over a disputed debt and disliked each other intensely. To realise that the same man had seduced his niece whilst a guest in his house simply fuelled his hatred and during the ferocious argument that followed Bass-Smith made an ominous threat—to reveal all he knew about the death of Edmonds's wife five years before unless, that is, Jeannette's belongings were handed over.

But Edmonds stood his ground and refused to hand over the goods. He determined, moreover, to discredit Bass-Smith in any way that he could. He began by trying to get him struck off the roll of surgeons for gross misconduct with a patient—further compounded by the fact that Jeannette was only seventeen at the time of the seduction and therefore below the age of consent. He then issued a writ for £586 (roughly equivalent to £17,000 today) which he declared was owed to him by the philandering doctor. Bass-Smith, in turn, tried to claim exorbitant fees for past, unclaimed medical services during Ann Edmonds's life-time, and when this failed he decided to file a petition for bankruptcy, rather than pay his debt to Edmonds. Not to be outdone, Edmonds announced that he intended to oppose the petition, which so infuriated Bass-Smith that he once more threatened to expose certain disturbing factors in the death of his adversary's wife.

With all the arrogance of the innocent Edmonds still refused to be intimidated and appeared in court the following January, against the doctor. Pushed to the limit, Bass-Smith wrote to Mr

Carter, the county coroner for Gloucestershire, expressing the view that Mrs Edmonds's death had not been a natural one—despite the fact that he had signed the death certificate indicating apoplexy as the cause.

Meanwhile, Jeannette, unable to stay with her mother, visited friends in Ross-on-Wye before going to stay in the doctor's home in London. What Mrs Bass-Smith felt about this arrangement can be imagined—indeed, within days Jeannette was homeless again and, having no means of support, she was literally destitute. In desperation she wrote to the Vicar of Newent, Rev Keene. His response was to find her a place in the St James's Diocesan Home, in Hammersmith, known locally as a Home For Unfortunates or Fallen Women; it was, in effect, a slightly better class of workhouse. No doubt guided by the reverend gentleman, Jeannette wrote to her uncle asking him to forgive her past indiscretion. At the same time the young lady, the essence of duplicity, was also confiding in Rev Keene; she told him of her conviction, which she shared with Matthew Bass-Smith, that her uncle had murdered his wife. Presumably the vicar informed Mr Carter, the county coroner, for he travelled to London to question Jeannette and, having already received a similar communication from the doctor, he ordered the exhumation of Mrs Edmonds's body, which had been buried some five years before.

The coroner's inquest into Mrs Edmonds's death was held at Gloucester Magistrates Court, on 14 February, 1872. One can imagine the interest that must have surrounded the enquiry as local people vied with each other for seats in the public gallery, eager to hear at first-hand the scandal in their midst—to learn the truth behind all the rumours that had spread about the Edmonds family which had hitherto held such a prominent position in the community. Rumours of death by violence, debt and subterfuge and, best of all, an illicit love affair between a married man of mature years and a young lady with some degree of social standing, but decidedly dubious morals.

And the spectators were not disappointed for the first witness to take the stand was none other than the young lady herself. Far from being cowed by her reduced circumstances and unenviable position, Jeannette openly admitted her affair with Matthew Bass-Smith and then proceeded to give her account of the events leading to the death of her aunt.

Edmund Edmonds was also called and gave his account of the night of 24 February, 1867. After saying good night to his dinner guests he had been preparing to make a journey to London but his wife didn't want him to go. She said that she was feeling unwell and begged him to stay at home with her. He was determined to go, however, and told her to go to bed. She then went upstairs to Aunt Polly's room, (which she shared with nine year old Oscar), and suddenly, saying that she was dying, she collapsed onto a trunk or travelling box by the side of the bed.

Dr Bass-Smith had been sent for and, although he lanced a large swelling on her temple, he was unable to save her life. Edmonds swore that he and his wife had not quarrelled that night; nor had he cursed or struck her, as some other witnesses were to testify. He further suggested that pique over the impending lawsuit had caused the doctor to contact the coroner so long after his wife's death. He went on to deny any suggestion of impropriety in his relations with his wife's younger sister, Polly, who had been living in his house for twelve years.*

Having heard all the evidence given on the first day of the inquest, including his own version of events, the police decided to arrest Edmonds, on suspicion of murder, without consulting the coroner. On the following day the coroner's jury decided that Mrs Edmonds's death had been caused by apoplexy, but, as this had, in their opinion, been brought about by her husband's violent behaviour, a charge of manslaughter was made against him. There was a great deal of antipathy towards Edmonds in the town and this was further compounded by a sermon preached by Keene on the following Sunday. As a result of his defamatory remarks about the moral aspects of the case and the ambiguous verdict of

---

* On 21 February 1872, Mrs Edmonds's brother, James Matthews, attempted suicide by cutting his throat. Probably the publicity of the case, the realisation that his sister may have been murdered, and the insinuations that his younger sister, Polly, had been engaging in an illicit affair with her brother-in-law, proved too much to bear.

manslaughter, the inquest witnesses were re-examined before magistrates and the charge changed to one of murder.

Understandably, for a man in his position, Edmonds found confinement in the local lock-up so distasteful that after the committal hearing he applied for bail. Surprisingly, despite the fact that he was detained on a murder charge, it was granted, in his own surety of £4,000 and further sureties set by the presiding magistrates who were, incidentally, very much opposed to his release.

On 19 March, free to orchestrate the best possible defence, Edmonds applied for his case to be heard, not at the Gloucester Assizes but at the Central Criminal Court of the Old Bailey, where he might expect an unbiased panel of jurors. Local prejudice against him was so strong, he pleaded, fuelled by scurrilous newspaper reports and the censorious sermon preached by Rev Keene, that he could not possibly expect a fair trial.

During the legal prevarication that followed this application Mr Justice Willes castigated Keene for the content of his sermon, which he considered 'unguarded and unfortunate in the circumstances', and granted Edmonds's request. The judge suggested, moreover, that the preacher might, in future, do well to restrict his references to vice, not from current events, but from the Bible, which, he felt, provided as rich a source as any.

The trial of Edmund Edmonds opened at the Old Bailey on 8 May, 1872, before the judge, Baron Bramwell. The prosecution was led by Mr Digby Seymour, QC, with Dr Kenealy, QC, assisted by Mr George Griffiths. Edmonds was defended by Mr Henry James, QC (who defended Florence Bravo in the famous 1876 poison case), aided by Messrs Huddleston, Griffiths and Browne. After the opening address for the prosecution, Edmonds was, for some reason never fully explained, allowed to leave the dock and sit at the solicitors' table so that he could 'communicate freely with his counsel.' Baron Bramwell voiced his disapproval by declaring that *any* prisoner would welcome such a privilege— one, incidentally, not extended to Armstrong at his subsequent trial. (A similar request *was* granted to the poisoner, Dr Palmer, of Rugeley, in 1856.)

Ann Bradd, who had been a maid in the Edmonds' household between 1864 and 1867, was called as the first witness for the prosecution. She reiterated the evidence she had given at the coroner's inquest, telling the court that she clearly remembered the day of her mistress's death—Sunday, 24 February. Ann Edmonds had seemed in good health and spirits, having entertained her dinner guests with a musical rendering of 'Too Late, Too Late!'

Shortly after eleven, when the dinner guests had left, the maid had heard the slam of the office door and seen Mrs Edmonds pacing about in the hallway. Soon after she had gone up to bed on the first floor she heard raised voices coming from the breakfast room. Realising that the solicitor and his wife were having a flaming row, she crept onto the landing to listen. The couple were 'having high words' and the quarrel seemed to be about a woman called Smallridge whom Mrs Edmonds suspected had entertained her husband on a recent visit to Gloucester. The maid heard her master shout at his wife to go to bed to which she screamed abuse at him, calling him a 'brute and a wretch'.

'Damn your eyes, go to bed!' came his reply, followed by the sound of some heavy object being hurled, hitting something and finally falling to the floor. This was followed by a loud scream from Mrs Edmonds as she ran from the room, pleading: 'There's a dear man, don't!' She said it three times. Still screaming and shouting she ran out into the garden, followed by her husband; she then came back into the house and ran upstairs to her sister's, Polly's, room. As her husband caught up with her she gasped: 'I am dying' and then asked Jeannette, who had been alerted by all the noise, to fetch her some water.

Questioned further, Ann Bradd said that when she next saw her mistress she was lying on the bed, tended by Polly and Dr Bass-Smith, and died soon afterwards. When questioned at the earlier coroner's court, the maid had said that she had often heard Edmonds and his wife quarrelling, that he often swore at her and wished her dead. In her opinion Mrs Edmonds had been struck by a candlestick in the breakfast room at the height of the row that night, and subsequently died of that injury. She said she had noticed that one of the candlesticks was bent at the top but had been asked not to say anything. But had she, perhaps, refused to keep quiet about the candlestick and all that she had heard that evening? She was clearly unhappy and gave in her notice soon after Mrs Edmonds's death—apparently over some spilled milk—but Polly had persuaded her not only to stay a little longer but also to promise never to mention the events of that Sunday night. Yet, despite the fact that when she did eventually leave, and Edmonds gave her an excellent reference, she had told him to his face that he was a bad man and would come to a bad end. Finally, the maid told the court that Ann Edmonds's mother, Mrs Matthews, had offered her 'hundreds of pounds' if she would say what really happened that night.

Next came the prosecution witness everyone wanted to see. Jeannette Helena Edmonds took the stand fully aware of the avid stares of the spectators filling every available seat in the court. The evidence she gave was vastly different from that given by Edmonds at the coroner's court. Only seventeen at the time of her aunt's death she recalled hearing Edmonds and his wife already quarrelling at seven o'clock on the evening of 24 February, although at supper time they 'seemed to be reconciled.' She was able to recall a number of occasions when the couple argued— mainly, she thought, because of her aunt's jealousy concerning her husband's associations with various female clients. But when asked about her uncle's relationship with Aunt Polly she considered the rumour to be unfounded—at least, during Mrs Edmonds's lifetime.

Questioned about the night of the murder, Jeannette said that she had gone to bed about half past ten and shortly afterwards heard her aunt and uncle arguing downstairs. She had come out of her room to see what was happening when Mrs Edmonds had run past her on the stairs, 'much agitated', and gone into Polly's room, carrying a candlestick. Her uncle had followed her into the bedroom in such 'a great passion' that her aunt had cowered on the other side of the bed.

'Jeannette, I am dying,' the poor woman wailed, to which Edmonds snarled, 'You be damned.' To this, his wife replied: 'I won't be damned.' This plucky, if foolish, response so enraged Edmonds that he rushed over to his wife and struck her on the side of her head with his clenched fist. According to Jeannette, the poor woman tried to stand up but sank onto a trunk by the side of the bed and, although she drank a little water, did not speak again.

When Dr Bass-Smith arrived he tried to ascertain what the patient had eaten that evening, clearly supposing she had been poisoned. For some reason, no one saw fit to inform the doctor that Mrs Edmonds had been attacked by her husband. Questioned about her affair with Dr Bass-Smith, Jeannette, far from affecting any maidenly reserve, told the court that the doctor often stayed as a guest in her uncle's house and used to come to her bedroom where they indulged in their 'illicit intercourse' undisturbed. They often spent nights together at various hotels and she was fully aware that the doctor was a married man, now with five children.

Under further cross-examination concerning her departure from Newent Jeannette did not falter at telling the court of her stay in the institution—'It's a Home for fallen women,' she said, without the slightest trace of embarrassment. When she finally stepped down from the witness box she was replaced by her lover, Dr Matthew Bass-Smith. Recalling the night of Mrs Edmonds's death he said that Edmonds had called to say that his wife had suffered a fit. While he was dressing he called back saying that if he, the doctor, did not hurry, she would be dead. When he arrived she was already unconscious and despite attempts to revive her by bleeding, applying a mustard poultice to her neck and hot water to her feet, she died shortly before one in the morning. While Edmonds was in the room, Bass-Smith had asked Aunt Polly if there had been 'any disturbance or violence' but her reply was negative.

Questioned further, the doctor told the court that after Mrs Edmonds's funeral—an occasion marked by many shops in the locality closing for the day—Edmonds had seemed depressed and inclined to blame himself for her death, saying that he had been less than kind to her during her lifetime. His place on the stand was taken by Dr Wilton, senior surgeon at Gloucester Infirmary, who had made a post-mortem examination of Mrs Edmonds's body. However, five years after burial the body was so decomposed that it was impossible to say with any certainty whether she had died from natural causes or as a result of a violent assault. He was able to determine, however, that there was no fracture of the skull but, in his opinion, a heavy blow to the head could have caused the attack of apoplexy that killed her.

According to *The Hereford Times*, Mr Huddleston addressed the court in tones of great indignation. The case for the defence, he said, 'required no arts of advocacy' as he was confident the jury would dismiss the charge and find that Mrs Edmonds had died naturally, from a fatal attack of apoplexy and not, as the prosecution suggested, from her husband's violence. He went on to taunt Dr Bass-Smith as being the instigator of the charge and referred to his client as a man of 'irreproachable character'. Regarding Jeannette, he said that it was now five years since her aunt's death and only now, after Edmonds had 'taken strong measures against the man who had corrupted' her, did she produce this trumped up story against him.

This said, the defence called Aunt Polly, in her proper name of Miss Mary Mathews. She refuted all that Jeannette, Dr Bass-Smith and the maid had said. Her version of the solicitor's household and the events leading to her sister's death was quite different. She had not, for instance, heard any quarrelling on the night of 24 February, nor the screams mentioned by the maid, Ann Bradd. She said that she had gone to bed after the dinner party leaving Edmonds, his wife and a clerk downstairs. She maintained that her sister, nine years her senior, had been unwell for at least a year before her death and suffered from headaches, frequent nose-bleeds and palpitations.

Far from running terrified from her husband that night Ann Edmonds was behaving normally, stopping, as was her habit, to have a few words with her son before retiring for the night. Polly did concede, however, that her sister had been trying to persuade Edmonds to forgo his trip to London but, she told the court, he had suggested she join him and, at the same time call on their eldest son, Edmund, who was studying at Cambridge. But Mrs Edmonds had dismissed this suggestion saying that she felt too ill. After sipping some water that Jeanette had brought her she said that she was dying. To this, according to Polly, Edmonds had cried: 'Oh, no!'

No blows or abusive language, she assured the court, had been exchanged the whole evening. To this she added that Dr Bass-Smith was not surprised by Mrs Edmonds's sudden death. He had always supposed, she said, that she would go like 'the snuff of a candle'. Finally, Polly strongly denied the allegation that she had told Jeannette, the maid or anyone else to keep quiet about a quarrel that night.

On the second day of the trial young Oscar Edmonds, now fifteen but aged nine at the time of his mother's death, took the stand and corroborated all that his aunt had said, at the same time denying that he had been coerced, in any way, by her or his father into appearing for the defence.

His testimony was followed by that of another maid, who, at the time of Ann Edmonds's death, had been Ann Cassidy; she had since married John Arch, who had been the Edmonds' groom. She, too, contradicted the evidence of earlier witnesses, in particular her fellow servant, Ann Bradd. She told the court that she had left the household nine months after Mrs Edmonds's death only on account of her marriage. She testified that the prisoner and his late wife had lived on the most affectionate terms. Her mistress, however, was often unwell during the last twelve months of her life and Dr Bass-Smith was 'always in attendance'. This remark must have caused a few sniggers amongst the spectators having already heard of the doctor's illicit activities whilst visiting the late Mrs Edmonds. She denied hearing any screams, abusive language or violence of any sort that evening.

Questioned further the maid said that when she saw Ann Bradd the following morning there was no mention of a quarrel and, she claimed, the first she heard of any violence being involved was at the Coroner's court. No candlestick was missing next day but, she had to admit, she had noticed that one was 'a little bent at the top'. In an effort to suggest that Mrs Edmonds had died naturally, peacefully even, she said she had seen no bruising or other marks on the body and even described Mrs Edmonds's corpse as having a 'pleasing look'.

Ann Arch was followed into the box by her husband, John, now employed as a railway signalman. He told the court he had been a groom at the Edmonds' house for two years before Mrs Edmonds's death and had been accustomed to driving her in the carriage. She was always delicate, he said, and used to tell him to drive slowly as she 'could not bear the the jolting of the carriage'. As far as he could see, Mr and Mrs Edmonds had lived 'very happily together and he treated her with much kindness. No one,' he went on, 'said anything about violence or a quarrel.' He was not surprised at the death for 'Mrs Edmonds herself always thought she would die suddenly.'

The defence also called a Mrs Symonds, who was employed as a governess from April 1855 until October 1866. She and her husband had been guests at the dinner party on the night Mrs Edmonds had died. The couple had behaved in their usual affectionate manner but Ann Edmonds had complained of feeling unwell and said she intended to speak to a doctor the next day. However, as the evening wore on she seemed to be better and more relaxed and even joined in the singing. Mrs Symonds had heard about the death the following morning and when she went to the house about 8 o'clock Jeannette had said nothing about any violence.

The cook, Mary Messenger, was called next and corroborated all that her fellow servant, Ann Arch, had said—she had seen and heard nothing on the night of 24 February and after her mistress had died nobody had mentioned violence of any kind.

As the trial progressed the jurors were faced with two distinctly different versions of events; the one given by Dr Bass-Smith, Jeannette and Ann Bradd and the other by Aunt Polly, Oscar, the governess and the three servants. Had the whole case, Edmonds's arrest and trial, been a malicious vendetta orchestrated by the exposed lovers, Bass-Smith and Jeannette? And did they enlist the help of the maid, Ann Bradd? Or were the villains of the piece the rest of that unhappy household—Edmonds himself, Polly, with whom he may have enjoyed an affair after his wife's death, as intimated by Jeanette, and even Oscar who saw his mother die? Which faction was telling the truth and which was lying? And if Jeannette, the doctor and the maid had suspected that it was the vicious blow from the candlestick that had killed Mrs Edmonds, why had they not said so at the time? It seems that everyone, whatever their doubts, had been prepared to keep quiet until, five years later, the discovery of the affair between Jeannette and the doctor had brought everything back into focus. Angry words, accusations and lies had broken the silence. Had Ann Bradd, in fact, been given notice because she'd said too much and did she, despite being allowed a further three months and a good reference, bear a grudge?

As for the other servants, had they been persuaded to keep quiet about the frequent rows between Edmonds and his wife? He had the perfect opportunity to tell them exactly what to say when they stayed with him for three or four days during the coroner's inquest. It must be remembered that in those days domestic servants were generally quite happy to do as they were told and not make trouble for themselves. After all, was it not common practice for a Victorian gentleman to chastise members of his family and staff within the privacy of his own home if he saw fit? Could it be that Edmonds, the distinguished looking man sitting alongside his counsel, a prominent citizen, a professional man, was also a martinet, a bully and a wife-beater in the privacy of his own home? Did he frequently abuse his wife, flaunt his infidelities and attack her, physically as well as verbally, on a number of occasions? And did the local people see through his veneer of middle class gentility—did they, perhaps, know him for what he was, a common wife-beater, a lecher and a man quite capable of murder? Was that the reason for his unpopularity? Did he deliberately murder his wife that Sunday night or did he, in a fit of temper at the height of their quarrel, fling the candlestick or use his fist and accidentally kill her?

Or was he, in fact, a much-maligned man who had taken his impoverished niece into his home, educated her and given her employment only to have his kindness abused by her scandalous affair with Matthew Bass-Smith? And finally, the most bitter calumny of all, to be accused of causing the death of his wife?

All these factors were meticulously addressed in the judge's summing up during which he urged the jury to attempt to disentangle the lies from the truth, a task that, he conceded, was made more difficult by the length of time that had elapsed since the murder. He reminded the jurors that it lay with the prosecution to prove the prisoner's guilt not the defence to prove him innocent. He urged them, therefore, that even if they felt that Edmund Edmonds *was* guilty, but the case had not been positively proved beyond a reasonable doubt, they must acquit him. This the jury did after just fifteen minutes' deliberation and he left the court an innocent man.

As far as is known, Edmonds continued to practice as a solicitor, despite the slur on his name that must have remained firmly imprinted on the collective memory of the people of Newent.

IX

Major Armstrong of Hay

At the centre of the story of Major Herbert Rowse Armstrong is the little market town of Hay which lies at the foot of the Black Mountains, on the right bank of the River Wye. Straddling the Welsh border it marks a point where three counties used to meet—Herefordshire to the east, Brecknockshire to the west and Radnorshire to the north. It is an unusual place, currently famous on two counts—the largest collection of secondhand books in the world and the still lingering interest in the Armstrong case.

Originally Hay was essentially a garrison town that had grown around the castle at its centre, and throughout the troubled times of the Middle Ages the inhabitants suffered appalling oppression as their lords settled their territorial disputes with enthusiastic thuggery.

By the time Hay had entered into the comparative peace of the Victorian age it had developed into a prosperous market town, attracting traders from all over Wales and the Midlands. This in turn spawned a plethora of local tradesmen to accommodate a flourishing local economy—numbering amongst them black-smiths, masons, carpenters, leather workers and weavers. With the population served by dozens of small shops catering for every need it had become a thriving, self-sufficient community. Inevitably, despite the temporary draw of market days, it also became somewhat inward looking and parochial.

It was in 1906, five years into the Edwardian era, that a diminutive young solicitor arrived in Hay, one who was to cause a sensation in the town and ensure its prominence in the annals of crime.

His name was Herbert Rowse Armstrong and he was to achieve the dubious distinction of being the only British solicitor to be hanged for murder.*

He was a small man, just five foot six and weighing a mere seven stones. One might describe him as dapper in appearance, fond of wearing high, starched collars and a flower in his lapel. In the fashion of the day he wore his moustache meticulously waxed. By nature he was mild-mannered, softly spoken, and extremely courteous; a stickler for form, the niceties of social intercourse and the maintaining of standards. Yet for all his pernickety ways he was popular in the town and commanded respect, having the upright carriage of a soldier. But perhaps his most striking features were his bright blue eyes which, though intent in their gaze, held the hint of a roguish twinkle.

Armstrong was born on 13 May, 1869, in Plymouth. His father, William Armstrong, was a colonial merchant and his mother, Eleanor, bore the maiden name of Rowse, which her son was to maintain throughout his life—it was also her name that he subsequently chose for his first born daughter. Amongst his parents' closest circle were Mr George Pearson Friend and his wife, Mary Anne Hollis, a strictly religious couple from nearby Teignmouth. They had two daughters and young Herbert and the girls became childhood friends. The elder of the girls was Katharine Mary, born in 1873. Her sister, Bessie Ida, was born two years later. By far the more outstanding intellectually, Katharine was very highly strung but physically weak and susceptible to falls, accidents and every childhood ailment. In 1902 a bicycle accident left her blind in one eye. The effect of her injury was hardly apparent except, perhaps, to lend a rather strained expression to her face. Shortly after the accident she had an attack of rheumatism in her left arm which reoccured at intervals throughout her life and in 1904 she had a severe attack of influenza which left her prone to catching colds and neuralgia. She was so sensitive that the least nervous excitement brought on bouts of sickness and she became a martyr to indigestion.

---

* Whilst Edmund Edmonds, in 1872, and Harold Greenwood, in 1920, were tried for the murder of their wives, both were acquitted.

Herbert Rowse Armstrong, when a solicitor in Hay

For all this, young Herbert formed a strong affection for Katharine which was to survive their separation when his parents moved to Liverpool. Possessing a keen intelligence, he rejected his father's profession and chose to study law at St Catherine's College, Cambridge; his studies were funded by the generosity of two maiden aunts who were anxious to assist their nephew's advancement. Their faith in him was rewarded for he worked hard, was a popular student and enjoyed university life. Gregarious by nature he made a number of firm friendships. One of these was with Charles Lisle Carr, who was to become Bishop of Hereford, and a loyal supporter of Armstrong to the end of his life.

Armstrong's small stature made him a natural choice to cox his college's rowing team and in his final year, to his immense pride, he coxed the 'Goldie' crew, understudies to the Cambridge eight who were to challenge Oxford in the Boat Race that year.

In 1891, Armstrong graduated with a Bachelor of Arts and settled for a career in law. Four years later, at the age of twenty-six, he was admitted as a solicitor with the Liverpool firm of Messrs Alsop, Stevens, Crooks and Co. and worked for them until 1901. It was during this period that he met Arthur Chevalier, another young solicitor, and they became life-long friends. He also developed an interest in the army and in May 1900 he was appointed to the rank of Second Lieutenant in the 1st Lancashire Royal Engineers. In November of that year he was proud to be promoted to full Lieutenant and this military side to his life continued to be of tremendous importance to him.

In 1901 he decided to move to Teignmouth where Katharine and Bessie were still living with their parents. He became a partner in the firm of Hutchins and Co. remaining with them for two years until the partnership was dissolved, whereupon he took over the Newton Abbott branch where he practiced on his own until 1906.

Whilst in Devon he continued his interest in the army. He joined the 1st Devon and Somerset Royal Engineers (Volunteers) and was promoted to Captain. He also renewed his friendship with Katharine, who, despite her inherent frailty and uncertain temperament, obviously attracted him with her unusual intelligence and effervescent manner of talking. They also shared a love of music and although her frequent bouts of rheumatism hindered her, she became a highly accomplished pianist. Even in her teens, Katharine, plagued by chronic constitutional problems, developed an interest in homeopathy; she was regularly taking pills prescribed for her by a Dr Piggott, of Teignmouth, and her life-long dependence on such remedies had already begun.

The relationship between Herbert and Katharine flourished and on 7 September 1905 they became engaged. In June 1906, Armstrong left Newton Abbot to join the firm of Edmund Hall Cheese, an ailing sixty-three year old solicitor with a solid practice in Broad Street, Hay, now Williams Beales & Co. His premises were directly opposite the offices of the only other solicitor

Hay's Broad Street, where the town's two solicitors
had offices opposite each other

in Hay, Robert Griffiths, also still a solicitors' office now run by
Gabb & Co.

At the time of Armstrong's appointment the firms were able to
co-exist quite amicably, finding sufficient custom to keep both
practices busy. He commenced work as Managing Clerk. It seems
that Mr and Mrs Cheese took an immediate liking to
Armstrong—he even lodged with them for a while—and after a
preliminary trial period of six months he was offered a partnership. He introduced £1,200 and acquired a half share in the business. It was a proud day for Armstrong when the name of the firm
was changed to Cheese & Armstrong and he felt that his prospects were sufficiently promising to enable him to marry
Katharine after an engagement of nearly two years. The marriage
took place at St James's Church, West Teignmouth, on 4 June,
1907. The bride was thirty-four years old and the groom thirty-
eight. A photograph taken on their wedding day shows Katharine
wearing a rather limp and shapeless frock, an image that suggests
that sensuality or high fashion were not amongst her priorities;
she is standing awkwardly, inclining slightly to the left where
Armstrong stands erect, smiling and looking well pleased.

After a short honeymoon in Switzerland the couple took up
residence at Rothbury, a well-apportioned house in Cusop, close

107

to the beautiful and secluded area on the outskirts of Hay known as The Dingle. It was a substantial house, built only two years earlier. As the Hay office was little more than a mile away they had no need of a motor car. Besides which, both Armstrongs enjoyed walking, so much so that Katharine often accompanied her husband into town in the morning and then met him again on his return in the evening. The new bride took her duties very seriously and, furthermore, considering herself to be an astute business woman, showed an unusual interest in her husband's work. Neighbours said later that they were a devoted couple and their relationship appeared to be amicable and affectionate, very much one of complementary equals. A year later, on 18 April, their first child was born—Eleanor Mary Armstrong.

Armstrong continued to work extremely hard and the business in Hay prospered. He had always enjoyed playing a full role in the life of the local community and became a churchwarden at St Mary's, in Cusop. He also joined the Freemasons, enrolling at the Hay Loyal Lodge, and, using his previous experience in the army, he set up D Company of the Brecknockshire Territorial Force in Hay. For recreation he enjoyed reading, listening to his wife playing the piano, gardening and the occasional game of lawn tennis.

On 20 February, 1912, when Katharine was nearly forty, the Armstrong's second child was born. This time it was a boy—Pearson Armstrong, who later acquired the nickname 'Sonny'—and by the end of that same year Armstrong and his expanding family moved into a much larger house closer to town. Mayfield was an impressive modern villa set back from the road behind a line of elegant cast-iron railings; it was one of the most spacious late-Victorian houses to be built in the vicinity and no expense had been spared in its construction. There were a number of outbuildings including a stable for two horses above which was a coach house to accommodate a groom. The house also had its own three acre paddock and substantial fruit and vegetable gardens. With its sweeping driveway, shrubbery, flower gardens and grandiose style Armstrong could feel that life was treating him well.

Mayfield

Armstrong was very much a family man—his wife and children were the mainstay of his life—though as a typical Edwardian husband Armstrong left the household management to his wife. Despite being apt to crumple under stress she nevertheless organised her three domestic staff efficiently—Emily Pearce, who had started as a nanny and, still called Nana, stayed on as a housekeeper, a maid, Harriet Price, recently widowed, and Lily Candy, an undermaid, later replaced by Inez Rosser. The garden, however, was Armstrong's responsibility and it became something of a preoccupation. Although he was able to employ a gardener, William Jay—and occasionally a jobbing gardener, the maintenance of the extensive grounds at Mayfield became a perpetual headache. Surrounded by open fields it fell prey to weeds, in particular that perennial scourge of all gardeners, dandelions. It was a constant battle to keep them under control, especially on the paths in the vegetable garden and along the driveway and Armstrong and Jay spent a great deal of time and effort trying to eradicate them. Before the war Jay had bought patent weedkiller on several occasions and at least managed to keep the situation under control. But with a wife as frugal as Katharine, and his own meticulous nature, Armstrong much preferred to make his own weedkiller as he considered patent preparations not only less effective but also far too expensive. He was also keen on chemistry and actually enjoyed the fiddly process involved, like an enthusiastic schoolboy experimenting with his chemistry set. Having found a likely recipe in a copy of *The Times*, he had torn it out and kept in his garden file in a small cupboard by the fireplace in the study.

On 2 May, 1914, he purchased a quarter pound of arsenic from John Frederick Davies, the chemist in High Town in Hay. (Still occupied by Hay's chemist shop, it is now called The Pharmacy, though greatly altered since Armstrong's day.) When making the sale, Davies asked Armstrong what he wanted arsenic for and was told the purpose. The chemist explained that he would have to tint the white arsenic with some colouring—either soot, charcoal or indigo—to prevent it being mistaken for a harmless powder such as salt, flour or bicarbonate of soda. In this instance, Davies tinted the arsenic with charcoal and asked Armstrong to sign the Sale of Poisons Book. It was a procedure he must have performed many times whilst serving other local gardeners with arsenic for precisely the same purpose.

Armstrong mixed the arsenic and caustic soda powders in equal proportions of four ounces each. He then made a concentrated solution by adding a gallon of water and boiling it on the kitchen range, using an old saucepan borrowed from Miss Pearce. How she must have resented the master invading her kitchen in high summer to fill the air with the revolting smell of hot caustic soda. He then poured this concentrate into an old port wine bottle and from this bottle the solution was diluted—one gallon of water to one tea-cup of weedkiller. For this messy and potentially dangerous operation he enlisted the help of Miss Pearce. All the contents were used on the weeds that afternoon and the empty bottle was put away in the loft above the stable and never brought back into the house. The unused caustic soda was put back in a tin and kept in the study cupboard, along with all the other gardening paraphernalia—including a rose spray and insecticide solution, normally used by Katharine, who took a particular interest in the roses.

Such was the pattern of life for Armstrong and his family—a fairly conventional existence in many ways, but comfortable. His involvement with the Masonic Loyal Hay Lodge and the Territorials, his appointment as Clerk to the Magistrates Court, and his regular attendance and wardenship of the parish church ensured a full professional and social life, one that guaranteed him the acquaintance of the most influential names in Edwardian Hay society. But in 1914, at the outbreak of world war, everything changed and events in Armstrong's life began to lead irrevocably towards disaster.

On 26 April 1914, Armstrong's partner, seventy-one year old Edmund Cheese, died of cancer of the prostate. The following day his wife died of a heart attack. This gave Armstrong the right to buy the remaining one half of the business and the brass plate was again changed, this time to: Herbert Rowse Armstrong, Solicitor. No sooner had this been done than Britain declared war on Germany. Forced to leave Edmund Cheese's nephew, A.C. Sampson, in charge of the office, Armstrong was posted to the south of England to join a contingent of the 1st Wessex Field Company, Royal Engineers, with the rank of Captain. He was engaged for the most part in administrative duties, where his meticulous eye for detail and rather pedantic attention to form was especially useful.

While Armstrong was away Katharine arranged the renting of Mayfield and went to live with her mother in Teignmouth, so that when posted to Bournemouth Armstrong was able to make frequent visits to her and the two children. Indeed, he only failed to spend his leave with her on one occasion—when he had to attend urgent business at his office in Hay. Somehow or other, with the help of Sampson, he managed to keep his business afloat. Similarly, across the road, the offices of Robert Griffiths were also struggling to survive. The old gentleman was far from well and his son, Trevor, set to succeed him, had been forced to suspend his legal studies and serve in France.

However, the impression is gained that Armstrong, despite his age, may have welcomed the change and even hoped to see some action. He was gregarious, not adverse to regimentation and had actively sought army life—he probably enjoyed the camaraderie, deference to rank and the freedom to enjoy a drink and a smoke, two pleasures strictly monitored at home.

In 1916 he was promoted to Major and later served the last three months of the war in France. Katharine worried constantly about Herbert and, fearful that he might be killed in action, made a will on 17 January, 1917, making the children—a third child, Margaret, was born in that year—the main beneficiaries. But Armstrong was fortunate to survive the war, finally returning to England in October 1918. Though officially retired from the army in 1921 he chose to retain his title of Major in civilian life. It was a matter of considerable pride and he became a familiar sight striding through the narrow streets of Hay, wearing riding breeches and his British Warm with the collar turned up, still very much a military man.

Once Katharine and the children were back at Mayfield Armstrong set to work to save his business by consolidating the clients he had left behind and attracting more. By this time the other solicitor, Robert Griffiths, had, in the absence of his son, Trevor, taken on a new man—one Oswald Norman Martin. This was the man who was to play a devastating role in the downfall of Major Armstrong. Oswald Martin was a thirty year old bachelor who, having been wounded in the jaw, was invalided out of the army. This injury had resulted in a partial paralysis of the right side of the face, which, in turn, caused him to have a quite discernible speech impediment. Originally from Tewkesbury, in Gloucestershire, where his brother was in the retail grocery business, he soon settled into Griffiths's office in Broad Street and it was here that he met Constance Davies, daughter of Fred Davies the chemist. She had been a nurse at the beginning of the war but ended up entertaining the troops in France. After the war, Constance had been employed as a typist by Robert Griffiths, and within weeks of her introduction to Oswald Martin, they became engaged to be married.

Previous writers on this case have insisted that Armstrong felt threatened by the arrival of Oswald Martin in the offices opposite. The facts of the matter, however, reveal that the reverse may well have been true. Far from seeing Martin as a dangerous and unforeseen rival, Armstrong always knew that either Robert Griffiths's son, Trevor, or another of the hundreds of young solicitors looking for work after demobilization, would one day join the other firm. Furthermore, far from attracting clients, Martin's presence across the road was, in fact, deflecting a number of Robert Griffiths's oldest clients, who preferred to deal with an established solicitor like Armstrong, who was well known and trusted locally, instead of with a relative youngster who was new to the area.

There was also something about Martin that put people off, a certain flashiness, perhaps, for in photographs he can be seen sporting a floppy bow-tie—definitely not pinstripe or cavalry twill. As for Constance, after their marriage she took to wearing luxuriant fox-furs, not just one but several layers of full pelts. This manner of dress, though very much in vogue for city dwellers, may have seemed a trifle theatrical for a typist in a small market town.

As to inappropriate dress, Mrs Armstrong had a great deal to say on that score. Not long after his engagement Oswald Martin received a formal invitation to tea at Mayfield. Two other guests, an army officer and his wife, were invited and Katharine was horrified when Martin arrived in casual dress—flannels and a sports jacket. It is difficult now to fully appreciate the emphasis ladies like Katharine Armstrong placed on traditional ceremonies like taking afternoon tea and being dressed accordingly. She was deeply offended by the mode of dress and Armstrong said later that 'Martin was never invited to the house again so long as my wife was alive.'

This incident and Katharine's exaggerated reaction illustrates the demarcation within the class system in Hay in the 1920's—it was clearly a case of knowing the class into which one was born and staying in it. By marrying a solicitor, Constance Davies and her family may have thought they could cross that invisible line between tradespeople and the professional class. What they did not realise was that Oswald Martin, despite his professional position, was still, in many eyes, 'in trade', like his brother and father-in-law.

It would appear that Fred Davies, in particular, felt this very deeply. He professed dislike for Armstrong and resented the fact that he had acted for another chemist, Mr Sant, when he set up a rival shop in the town—which, although not licensed to dispense medicines, was proving very popular. Judged by his photographs and subsequent actions Davies seemed to have been a rather sour-faced and insular man; yet he saw himself as somebody in the town, a man of substance and a force to be reckoned with—he was, after all, a qualified chemist who had worked in Hay for forty years, dispensed his own medicines and had been, like Armstrong, a Freemason. Yet he was not accepted on an equal footing socially and he resented it bitterly.

During the war, Jay, the gardener at Mayfield, had done his best to control the weeds using patent weedkillers but when the Major returned he was exasperated to see how overgrown the garden had become in his absence. The paths and especially the drive were once more completely smothered with weeds. Before the war he'd even got Miss Pearce and Harriet Price weeding on their hands and knees, a laborious task and not very effective when dealing with the more tenacious, tap-rooted plantains growing in the lawn.

He now renewed his battle, determined to eradicate the weeds once and for all. In June 1919, intent once more on using his special recipe he bought half a pound of arsenic and some caustic soda from Fred Davies's shop and signed the Sale of Poisons Book. He used half of this packet and put the remainder in a tin next to the caustic soda in the cupboard in the study.

Life seemed, at least, a little brighter. The country, no longer at war, had begun to recover from its gloom; there was a new optimism and Armstrong was happy to be back in the fold of his family. His eldest child, Eleanor, was now eleven years old and attending a boarding school in Malvern whilst Katharine taught

Pearson at home, giving him lessons in the study every morning. The youngest child, Margaret, was now a bright, vivacious four year old, and a great favourite with everyone.

As for Katharine, she supervised her household, entertained selected neighbours to tea, involved herself with church matters, especially missionary work, and tended the roses. She read a great deal—Armstrong referred later to her 'literary pursuits'— and enjoyed playing the piano for her family and guests. But like many women raised in excessively religious families, with its stultifying atmosphere of repression, Katharine was prone to moods of self-loathing, doubt and recrimination. At times she could be strong-willed, dogmatic, and acutely introspective, yet she was easily excited, demonstrating her nervousness in frenetic chattering.

She had also become a hypochondriac, and, having little faith in doctors, continued to dose herself with a veritable arsenal of homeopathic remedies. But when, in 1919, she developed pains in her right shoulder and arm—accompanied by some numbness in her fingers—she was sufficiently worried to consult Dr Hincks. His surgery was in Broad Street, opposite the town clock, and just up the road from her husband's office. Tom Hincks was a large, country squire type of man and was, as his father before him, extremely popular. People trusted Hincks and converged on his surgery, especially on market days; harassed mothers came in from the outlying farms with their menfolk and livestock, dragging along their unhealthy brood—some with rickets, some with hacking coughs, others with scabies and squints and all manner of complaints, convinced that if anyone could sort them out, Tom Hincks could. Whether he was, in fact, as competent and good natured as local people believed is debatable but he was certainly a hardworking man, in the saddle for many hours each week, visiting patients living in the more inaccessible hill farms.

Knowing that Mrs Armstrong had a history of rheumatism, Hincks diagnosed brachial neuritis. This condition gradually improved, though she was rarely completely free of its effects.

It was in July the following year that Armstrong alleged that Katharine made a new will, leaving the bulk of her estate to him.

This was, in fact, invalid, for it was written in Armstrong's hand and, it was later proved, his wife's signature was a forgery. Yet Miss Pearce later testified that when she was called to witness the document she signed her name in the presence of both Mr and Mrs Armstrong. However, the second witness, the young maid Lily Candy, was not present; when questioned she insisted that she signed the document in the library at Mayfield on a quite separate occasion, when only Major Armstrong was present.

A month later, in August 1920, Katharine began to feel unwell. She was under considerable stress having to cope with all three children at home for the summer holidays without the help of Emily Pearce, who had taken a month's leave. It was all too much for her and she cracked under the strain, becoming deluded and depressed.

Armstrong, worried by his wife's irrational behaviour and rest-lessness at night—she had taken to wandering about downstairs, imagining people were moving around outside and staring at her through the windows—asked Dr Hincks to prescribe a sleeping draught for her. He brought her a bunch of violets and did every-thing he could for her—even asking his daughter to watch her carefully during the day and report back to him in the evenings. But she did not improve and on a subsequent visit to Mayfield on 20 August, Dr Hincks could see that Katharine was not being simply neurotic but was suffering from a serious mental distur-bance. On examination he detected a mitral murmur of the heart and, having taken a urine sample, found traces of albumen, usually a symptom of underlying kidney damage or disease.*

The following day Armstrong sent for his wife's sister, Bessie, and Arthur Chevalier, now a family friend for many years. There was a family conference during which Dr Hincks suggested that Katharine should be admitted to a private asylum, Barnwood House, near Gloucester, where his own sister had recently been treated. It was also agreed that, as Katharine was potentially a suicide risk, the Major's razors and service revolver should be securely stored. In Hincks's opinion, Katharine's mental insta-

---

* It was suggested later that Katharine may have suffered from Addison's Disease.

bility was probably due to the menopause; she was, after all, forty-seven at the time and of a nervous, melancholic disposition. Dr Jayne, from Talgarth, was called to give a second opinion; he found Katharine distressed and rambling, and suffering from the delusion that she had lived an ungodly life, had treated her children cruelly and had frequently defrauded the tradesmen—which she had never in fact done. After further discussion with the family it was decided that Katharine be certified insane.

Whilst Katharine was at Barnwood she was treated for a month with a tonic containing arsenic, and slowly improved. Armstrong visited her every two weeks as advised by the hospital doctor and on each occasion Katharine begged her husband to take her home—she hated Barnwood and missed her children dreadfully. By January 1921, five months after her admission, her doctor reluctantly agreed that Katharine had improved sufficiently to be allowed home in the care of her husband and a local nurse, Gladys Kinsey, though he felt the move a little premature. He was soon proved right—she continued suffering delusions, was physically weak and was so depressed that at times she appeared to harbour thoughts of suicide for, soon after her return, she asked the nurse whether a fall from the attic window would be sufficient to kill someone. So convinced did Gladys become that Katharine would try to commit suicide that she asked the Major if he could send for a properly trained psychiatric nurse. Equally concerned for his wife's health, he obtained the services of Eva Allen from Cardiff. In addition he told the maids to be especially vigilant.

Winter that year had been particularly wet and mild; Armstrong, probably intending to get the place tidied up before his wife's home-coming, and forgetting that he already had some arsenic left over in the cupboard, bought another quarter pound from Fred Davies's shop on 11 January. He said later it had been his intention to use it that weekend but, feeling unwell and confined to bed*, he put it away in the cupboard, still wrapped and tied with string. He placed it on top of the tin of caustic soda,

---

* Although it was never established that Major Armstrong had the disease, Dr Hincks was treating him for suspected syphilis at this time.

unopened and therefore unaware that John Hird, the chemist's assistant, having forgotten to tint it with charcoal, had inadvertently sold him white arsenic. It was a foolish mistake and one that adds to the conundrums surrounding the case.

On 8 February, Mrs Armstrong celebrated her forty-eighth birthday, which was to be her last. On 13 February she was sick after eating Sunday lunch of mutton followed by bottled gooseberries with the rest of the family. The following day a neighbour called to see Katharine; although Miss Pearce was in the house, the nurse was off duty for a couple of hours, and Katharine was sitting on the veranda, wrapped in a shawl and obviously unwell.

On 16 February, Katharine had given Pearson his usual lesson in the study, (during which she had become annoyed at having to waste time looking for his lost exercise book)—but after lunch she was again taken ill, complaining of acute dyspepsia. The previous day Nurse Allen had taken away the homeopathic pills Katharine had always taken for indigestion; instead she gave her some bicarbonate and water. This offered some temporary relief but when her condition worsened Armstrong sent an urgent message to Dr Hincks. On examination the doctor found that Katharine's skin was discoloured and, once she had also suffered bouts of severe vomiting, he declared that she was 'very acutely ill'.

Hincks then visited daily, but her condition continued to deteriorate. Subject to continual vomiting she became emaciated and spent most of her time in bed. Just how mobile Katharine was during the last six days of her life was to become a point of crucial importance. She kept most, if not all, of her homeopathic medicines in a small, unlocked chest on the mantelshelf, about three or four feet from her bed. Both Dr Hincks and Nurse Allen knew that Katharine was taking her own medication but after a cursory check on 15 February, neither bothered to inspect the medicine chest or monitor what their patient was taking. The nurse later confirmed that Katharine continued using her own medicines right up until Monday 21 February, by which time she was very seriously ill and, by all accounts, too weak to get out of bed. On that morning Nurse Allen left her for at least an hour while she walked to Dr Hincks's surgery in Hay to fetch some nutrient suppositories. After a restless night in the care of a relief nurse, it was clear that Mrs Armstrong was dying; by nine o'clock in the morning, after a brief conversation with her husband, she lost consciousness. Unable to help in any way and led to believe by Dr Hincks that she could last the day, Armstrong accepted the offer of a lift and went into Hay to catch up on some work. Katharine Armstrong died a few minutes after he reached his office.

The funeral, on Friday 25 February, at St Mary's, Cusop, was a small affair attended by Bessie Friend, Arthur Chevalier and a few close friends. The wording on the wreath from Major Armstrong and his children read 'From Herbert and the Chicks'.

In the month following his bereavement Armstrong became ill and depressed. Amongst others, he received a letter of sympathy from a long-time friend, Marion Gale; she was a kindly, middle-aged widow who, with her elderly mother, had befriended Armstrong when he was stationed in the West Country during the war. Before taking the advice of Dr Hincks to take a short holiday in Sicily he saw Marion during a business trip to London. In May that year he asked her to marry him—spurred on, perhaps, not from any great passion but the need to find a sympathetic companion and housekeeper who would help share the burden of raising his three young children.

While Marion considered his proposal Mayfield remained empty during the early summer of that year. With the children still at school and Miss Pearce on holiday it was a lonely time for the Major; he went to stay with his neighbours across the road, Mr and Mrs Tunnard Moore. It was at this time that he decided to tackle the dandelions once more and divided half of the arsenic he'd bought in January into separate paper sachets. Armed with these, and using an old chisel to make an incision into the roots of the most stubborn weeds, he dropped the arsenic directly into the hole he had made, thus killing the weed at the root without damaging the surrounding grass.

Taking advantage of the children's absence, he went over to Mayfield and proceeded to make a score or more sachets, each

The study at Mayfield with its bureau

containing a few grains of arsenic. He said later that it was only at this point, when he opened the packet in the cupboard, that he realised that he had been sold *white* arsenic. He said he also noticed that the string, which had been secure when he put the packet away, had been untied. Unaware of any significance in this and not wishing to create trouble for Fred Davies's assistant he said nothing. He spent the afternoon happily killing off weeds, at the end of which he was unaware that there was one sachet left amongst the other bits and pieces in the pocket of his gardening jacket. As he had only used half of the arsenic he placed the remaining two ounces, still in the original paper, in a drawer in his bureau.

Having had to cope with the loss of his wife and organise the children's schooling it was time for Armstrong to settle down to business once more. He and Oswald Martin were soon to cross swords over a land purchasing deal, one of some duration and complexity. This involved the sale of a mansion known as Velinnewydd and a number of tenanted farms, on behalf of the owner for whom Armstrong was acting. These had been offered by auction at Brecon, the sale being interrupted by the angry tenant farmers, Martin's clients, violently opposed to the sales. Eventually matters reached a point where tempers became frayed, contracts were withdrawn and the return of the deposits demanded. Despite this, the two solicitors were on fairly cordial terms professionally; Martin would occasionally borrow books from Armstrong's excellent library and always maintained that he found him courteous and helpful. Nevertheless, he professed to be a little surprised when, at the height of the conflict over the contract, Armstrong invited him to tea at Mayfield on Wednesday, 26 October. Armstrong, despite his Masonic and business matters, was still lonely after his wife's death and welcomed visitors in the evening, many being invited to tea. The meal, consisting of a pot of tea, scones and currant bread, had been prepared by the housekeeper, Miss Pearce, and, after a stroll round the garden, the two men ate in the drawing room.

Martin later insisted that Armstrong passed him a buttered scone* with the words 'Excuse my fingers'. Martin was surprised, as he tucked into several slices of buttered currant loaf, that Armstrong did not bring up the business of the sale, as he assumed this was the reason behind the invitation. Instead the two talked generally about the pressure of work and staff shortages before parting at six-thirty.

Later that evening, after eating supper of jugged rabbit and crème caramel with his wife, Martin was taken ill with severe pains in his stomach and prolonged bouts of vomiting. When called, Dr Hincks diagnosed a bilious attack brought on by over-work and lack of exercise and prescribed bismuth.

The following morning, however, Fred Davies, discussing his son-in-law's illness with Hincks said that, in his opinion, Martin had been poisoned. It must be remembered that less than eighteen months before, another solicitor, Harold Greenwood, from Kidwelly, near Carmarthen, had been tried and acquitted of the

---

* Miss Pearce, who baked the scones, and Harriet Price, who served tea that day, said that the scones were uncut and unbuttered. The three scones left over were put back in a tin and eaten later by the maids.

murder of his wife with arsenic. The case, which had been widely reported, had become a favourite topic of conversation in Hay. The verdict was generally regarded with scepticism and there can be little doubt that the case had done much to fuel Davies's suspicions concerning the recent death of Mrs Armstrong.

So convinced was he that she had been poisoned and so virulent was his animus towards his son-in-law's rival that he couldn't resist telling Hincks of his suspicions. The doctor was initially reluctant to go along with this preposterous theory and continued to treat his patient for a billious attack. But then, on 30 October, Davies showed him a box of chocolates—two of which showed signs of being tampered with—and told him that the chocolates had been sent anonymously through the post to Oswald Martin on 20 September. The sender, he was sure, was Armstrong. He and Constance had eaten a couple and then put the box away until a small dinner party on 8 October. One of their guests that evening was Martin's sister, Dorothy; she had eaten one of the chocolates, which Constance had set out into sweet dishes as a dessert. That night, Davies went on, Dorothy had been taken very ill with vomiting and diarrhoea. Taking into account the two incidences of sickness, Hincks agreed to take a sample of Martin's urine for analysis. This was done the following day, under far from sterile conditions. Davies produced an empty bottle, which had contained hydrogen peroxide, from a cupboard in his dispensary, and Martin's urine sample, along with the suspect chocolates were parcelled up and sent to the Clinical Research Association in London.

The analysis, made for the Home Office by Dr John Webster, established that there were traces of arsenic in the urine sample and in two of the chocolates, which had definitely been tampered with. On the strength of these results, the Director of Prosecutions ordered an immediate investigation which culminated two months later in the arrest of Major Armstrong on a charge of the attempted murder of Oswald Martin.

The arrest was made at Armstrong's office shortly after ten o'clock on Saturday, 31 December, 1921, by Albert Weaver, Deputy Chief Constable of Herefordshire, and Chief Inspector

Alfred Crutchett of New Scotland Yard. Shocked but co-operative, Armstrong made a voluntary written statement and even offered to accompany the police officers to Mayfield where he said he would show them where to find his stock of arsenic. It was at this point that a fatal mistake was made—he forgot about the remaining two ounces of the white arsenic which he had put in the drawer of the bureau. It was only when, a little later, he was formally arrested and asked to turn out the pockets of his gardening jacket and saw the small packet of arsenic left over from his last attempt on the dandelions, that he remembered the arsenic in the bureau. He also realised that the police would find it there but, having initially omitted to mention it, saw that he was in a very awkward position. He did the only thing possible—he told his solicitor, T.A. Matthews.

To further compound the dilemma the police made two subsequent searches at Mayfield but failed to find the white arsenic and it was only on Matthews's second visit, in the company of Dr Ainslie, that the arsenic was found, wedged in the back of a drawer. Expecting the police to find it eventually, Matthews decided, perhaps with hindsight unwisely, to put it back in the bureau and to say nothing.

On the following Monday morning Armstrong had to bear the shame of appearing in the tiny courthouse in Hay, where he was still officially Clerk to the Magistrates. On hearing the charge against him his manner remained calm; he even went out of his way to help the elderly gentleman who had replaced him as clerk. He stood to attention when charged, neatly dressed and sporting a bright red tie for the occasion. He was remanded in custody pending further investigations, no doubt painfully aware that news of his arrest had probably already spread throughout the town. It had, and as he was escorted from the building there were cheers of support and someone called 'Three cheers for the Major!'

Dr Hincks, at first dubious of any suspicion against Armstrong, with whom he had been on friendly terms, now turned against him. He told the police that he thought Katharine Armstrong had died, not of gastro-enteritis, but from arsenical poisoning. An order was obtained on 2 January for the exhumation of her body which was examined by Bernard Spilsbury, considered to be the most experienced morbid pathologist of the day.* The corpse was taken from the churchyard of St Mary's to nearby Church Cottage, where the windows had been boarded up to frustrate the ghoulish attentions of the onlookers. But little could be seen for it was already dark and Humphrey Webb, the undertaker, and his son had to work by lantern light. A young lad was sent down to Hay for a bottle of whisky to fortify the men in their grisly work and on his return he happened to see into the room where the body had been laid out on wooden trestles. He was shocked to see that Mrs Armstrong was still recognisable nearly a year after her burial, even down to the bows of ribbon on the end of her plaited hair.*

A detailed analysis of specimens taken from the body showed that, as Fred Davies had suspected, there was arsenic in virtually every part of Katharine Armstrong's body, more than nine and half grains, and it was deemed that her husband, now on remand in Worcester Gaol, was responsible.

At the resumed Magistrates' hearing in the little courthouse at Hay, Armstrong was further charged with the murder of his wife. He had to suffer the added ignomy of hearing Martin and Davies give evidence against him. The servants at Mayfield were also questioned at some length; so, too, were Bessie Friend and Arthur Chevalier. Having heard the testimony of a number of witnesses the magistrates decided that there was a case to answer and ordered that Armstrong stand trial at the next Hereford Assizes for the murder of his wife and the attempted murder of Oswald Martin.

The presiding Assize judge was seventy-three year old Mr Justice Darling, a controversial figure, considered a wit with literary aspirations; it was to be his last murder case before his

* Sir Bernard Spilsbury; Senior Home Office pathologist: much feared as a prosecution witness—he was cool, precise and unshakable. After a series of family bereavements, he killed himself in 1947.
* The presence of arsenic in a body, whether ingested or through seepage or migration from surrounding soil, can act as a preservative.

retirement.* As in all major poison cases the role of prosecutor was taken by the Attorney General, in this instance, Sir Ernest Pollock. He was assisted by a formidable medical team—in addition to Bernard Spilsbury, there were Sir William Willcox, physician, and Dr John Webster, Senior Analyst at the Home Office—all three were considered experts in their field.

Defending Armstrong against this prestigious panel was Sir Henry Curtis Bennett, KC; whilst undoubtedly an imposing figure and a most able advocate, he lacked the fire and dramatic impact of Marshall Hall, the successful defender of Greenwood at Carmarthen, who had been approached as defence counsel for Armstrong, but was unwell and unable to accept the brief. Curtis Bennett was backed by three excellent but far from eminent physicians—Drs Toogood, Stead and Ainslie.

The trial, which opened on 3 April, 1922, at the Shire Hall in Hereford, lasted for ten days and excited immense interest, not just locally but nationally. Despite the harsh weather, there had been a recent fall of snow, vast crowds gathered outside the court to watch the daily comings and goings of the legal dignitaries and, of course, to catch a glimpse of Major Armstrong. For the occasion he was wearing his brown tweed suit, spats and brown boots—which he always cleaned himself—and his moustache was elegantly waxed.

The first charge related to the murder of Katharine Armstrong and the judge, despite the adamant objection of Curtis Bennett, ruled that the evidence relating to the second charge of attempted murder of Oswald Martin when he visited for tea, should be admissible.* This evidence, Curtis Bennett was sure, though

---

* Sir Charles Darling; became a judge at 47 years of age. He was renowned for his courtroom wit and, like George Hardinge in the Mary Morgan case, liked to compose verse, some of which was published in various legal magazines. During his career at the Bench he was involved in many of the most famous trials, including Frederick Seddon, Steinie Morrison, George Smith and Dr Crippen. He died in 1936, aged 87.

* A Grand Jury dismissed a third charge of attempting to murder Oswald Martin by poisoned chocolates on the grounds that *there was no evidence to suggest that Armstrong had sent them.* Despite this, the jury must have known of the chocolates, if only from newspaper articles.

Nurse Kinsey, Miss Rosser, Nurse Lloyd, Miss Pearce and Mrs Price

purely circumstantial, would prove highly prejudicial to the prisoner. The cases for both prosecution and defence were to rely
largely on medical evidence.

However, as a close study of the trial will confirm, Mr Justice
Darling was quite openly biased in favour of the prosecution's
theory.* He conspicuously elevated the testimony of the Home
Office experts with sycophantic introductions whilst doing his
utmost to belittle the defence doctors by his disparaging
comments throughout the proceedings. He openly ridiculed
Armstrong's defence, and towards the end of the trial, when the
cross-examination was complete—and, it must be said, when the
case for the defence looked most plausible—he ordered

---

* A full account of the trial may be found in *The Notable British Trials*
series, edited by Filson Young.

Armstrong to remain in the witness box and proceeded to submit him to an onslaught of invective. He questioned him unremittingly about the white arsenic found in the back of the bureau and about the little packet found in his coat pocket. It was during this interrogation that Armstrong, having previously taken the stand for nearly six hours and answered questions with calm courtesy, began to show signs of stress, a time during which Curtis Bennett would have been powerless to intervene. He seemed to lose his customary confidence, became almost inarticulate and his answers lacked conviction. When he was finally allowed to leave the witness-box the damage to his credibility was irreparable.

In his summing up, Mr Justice Darling strongly recommended the jury to accept the prosecution's view that Katharine Armstrong was being slowly poisoned before she went to Barnwood and that the fatal dose of arsenic must have been given to her within twenty-four hours of her death—at a time she was supposedly incapable of taking it herself. He dismissed entirely the theory proposed by the defence doctors that all the symptoms presented by Mrs Armstrong before she went to Barnwood were due to auto-intoxication—an accumulation of 'natural' poisons that had built up in her body, producing symptoms such as constipation, neuritis, rheumatoid arthritis and chronic indigestion. In addition, that the albumen in the urine and the condition of the heart may have been caused similarly. The judge failed to address the fact that if Mrs Armstrong had already been criminally poisoned the use of a tonic containing arsenic in the asylum would have caused her condition to deteriorate, not improve.

Convinced that Katharine had been suicidal, the defence doctors had suggested that she had taken a large dose of arsenic some days before her death—probably on 16 February—some of which had become encapsulated and attached itself to mucous in the wall of the stomach. They also acquainted the jury with the fact that arsenic, like most poisons, was capricious by nature and variable in its effects. Indeed, although a minimum fatal dose was generally acknowledged to be between two or three grains there had been many recorded cases of patients living for several days after taking massive doses. It was the opinion of the defence that the duration of Katharine Armstrong's last illness would suggest a case of encapsulated arsenic, which was not uncommon. Having taken a fairly large dose, part had become encysted and for a while attached itself to the wall of the stomach, later to dissolve and pass down into the bowel, ultimately causing her death.

As to the three-hundredths of a grain of arsenic found in Oswald Martin's urine, the defence reminded the jury that Martin had been taking bismuth for four or five days prior to giving the urine sample. Bismuth was notoriously susceptible to arsenic contamination, a point not contested by the Crown. In addition, the urine sample was taken in an amateurish manner and in far from sterile conditions, (which would undoubtedly invalidate the result today), and the bottle used had previously contained hydrogen peroxide, another substance prone to harbour arsenical impurities. Furthermore, urged the defence, the bottle had been stored in a cupboard in Davies's dispensary alongside numerous other bottles, some of which would have contained other noxious substances. These perfectly valid points were derided by the judge in his summing up and the jury were left in little doubt as to where his own convictions lay.

At various times, whilst listening to Darling's closing speech, which lasted four hours, Armstrong, according to a local reporter, was seen to be balancing a copy of the Bible on which he had sworn before giving evidence, on its spine along the front of the dock, and catching it each time it was about to fall.

At the start of the trial Curtis Bennett had been absolutely convinced that, when dealing with the murder charge, the evidence concerning the tea-party at Mayfield was inadmissible; he therefore conducted, erroneously in retrospect, a purely passive defence, content that the Crown could not prove beyond reasonable doubt that Armstrong had given arsenic to his wife. One cannot help feeling that had Marshall Hall conducted the defence the jury could probably have been convinced that Katharine *did* take a fatal dose of white arsenic herself, either accidentally mistaking it for, perhaps, bicarbonate of soda, or with the clear intention of taking her own life. She was, after all, depressed, fearful and very confused at the time.

Major Armstrong in the dock at the Shire Hall, Hereford. Mr Justice
Darling presiding, Sir Henry Curtis Bennett in profile in foreground

The jurors left the court to consider their verdict at eight
minutes to five in the afternoon. So confident was Curtis Bennett
of an acquittal, despite the judge's behaviour, that he went for a
walk only to be told that the jury, after just forty minutes' deliberation had returned a verdict of guilty on the charge of murdering
his wife. He was absolutely shattered by his defeat. He told a
reporter 'I have been in forty-eight murder trials, for and against,
and I have never known the verdict so open.' At a later date he
was to refer to the trial as 'unjust' and a 'poor show'.

It came as no surprise, however, that Mr Justice Darling told
the stunned court that he totally concurred with the verdict and
renounced any suggestion that Katharine Armstrong had
committed suicide. Telling Armstrong that he had been given 'a
fair trial' and been 'brilliantly defended' he proceeded to
sentence him to death.

Afterwards, the foreman of the jury told the press that they had
convicted Armstrong on the grounds that firstly, they accepted the
prosecution's view that Katharine Armstrong had been given the

arsenic within twenty-four hours of her death, and secondly, they did not believe the Major's explanation for the presence of the little packet of arsenic in his pocket at the time of his arrest. Huge crowds of onlookers and reporters, many of whom were convinced of Armstrong's innocence, and therefore shocked and angered by the guilty verdict, watched in silence as the car took him back to Gloucester Gaol. One reporter noticed that the Major, huddled in the back seat, was quietly weeping.

Curtis Bennett was not the only one to be devastated by the verdict. So, too, was Tom Matthews who had worked tirelessly in Armstrong's defence. He received numerous letters of support, including many from gardeners willing to testify that they used similar devices to Armstrong to kill off individual weeds. Various newspapers and journals took up the argument and many expressed dissatisfaction, not only with the verdict, but with many aspects of the trial—in particular the blatant bias of the judge. The popular crime writer, Edgar Wallace, protested angrily in an article published in *John Bull* on 15 April, emphasising the fact that the prosecution did not even know about the white arsenic in the bureau until told by the defence, even if belatedly. He also protested that there was nothing odd about a man going to the trouble of killing the roots of individual weeds with arsenic. 'I knew a man in Africa,' he wrote, 'who used to carry a little phial of nicotine to destroy certain flies that pestered his roses. If some of us,' he went on, 'were on trial for our lives and our eccentricities were produced against us, I daresay that they would seem even more absurd than Armstrong's.'

Harold Greenwood also wrote an emotive article in the following week's issue of the same magazine in which he commiserated with the fate of Armstrong. His sincerity, however, was a little suspect, for he also wrote several unpleasantly avaricious letters to Armstrong himself, trying to act as broker for a newspaper that wanted to publish an article written by Armstrong as he awaited execution.

But an appeal was lodged and during the hearing, which lasted three days, Curtis Bennett, in a last desperate attempt to save his client, spoke for twelve hours; he vehemently protested against the admissibility of the Oswald Martin evidence, despite the fact that this seemed to be of little relevance in why the jury reached its decision, and demanded that the verdict should be quashed. But he was over-ruled on the grounds that, even without it, there was sufficient alternative evidence to render the conviction safe. The appeal was dismissed on 16 May and the sentence of death remained.

The warders who were with Armstrong during his last days found him to be a man of courage and courtesy and one deeply concerned for his children. His last hours were spent in writing letters of thanks to his friend and solicitor, Tom Matthews, and also to the Rev J.J. de Winton, vicar of Hay, who were both convinced of his innocence. He made all the necessary arrangements for the care of his children, nominating Arthur Chevalier as their legal guardian. He also bestowed various small gifts to those who had been kind to him throughout his ordeal.

Herbert Rowse Armstrong was hanged at Gloucester Gaol on 31 May 1922 at eight in the morning. Thousands had signed a petition for a reprieve and such was the interest in the case a vast crowd had gathered since daybreak. So slight was his frame that John Ellis*, the public executioner, provided an extra long drop of eight feet eight inches to ensure there was sufficient pull on the rope to dislocate his neck. Armstrong maintained his innocence to the end, but accepted his fate and walked to the scaffold unaided.

That Katharine died of arsenical poisoning there can be no doubt but the central question is whether Armstrong gave it to her or she took it herself. Armstrong was convicted on purely circumstantial evidence, for no-one saw him give his wife arsenic. He bought the arsenic quite openly, unlike most known poisoners, and as for trying to poison Oswald Martin, surely he would not have used poison bought form his intended victim's father-in-

---

* John Ellis, a barber by profession, chief executioner from 1916 to 1923. Formerly assistant to Henry Pierrepoint, who disliked him. He retired soon after his execution of Edith Thompson in 1923. Ellis was a heavy drinker and, after a suicide attempt in 1924, succeeded in killing himself a year later.

law, a shrewd and suspicious man who already disliked him intensely?

More significantly, knowing the outcome of the Greenwood case, in which the exhumation of Mabel Greenwood's body led to her husband's arrest for murder, surely Armstrong, if he had poisoned Katharine, would have taken the extra precaution of having her body cremated, or at least not created additional risk of discovery by attempting a second murder? It is also worth noting when considering this case that the hallmark of the clever poisoner is to isolate the intended victim from his or her family and limit medical intervention as much as possible. Armstrong did neither—in fact, quite the reverse. As soon as Katharine became ill he sent for her sister and a family friend and pestered Dr Hincks to come to the house every day to monitor her illness; he even employed a full-time psychiatric nurse to care for her and urged the whole household to be more vigilant. It is also remarkable that, after Katharine's death, Armstrong, if he had something to hide, did not at once insinuate that she had committed suicide. In the circumstances, this would have been accepted as a sad, but wholly plausible outcome of Katharine's tragic decline into mental instability.

And what of the motive? The Major had not touched the small amount of money he inherited from the second will and as for his relationship with Marion Gale, even Mr Justice Darling was unable to suggest it was anything other than friendship at the time of Katharine's death.

There are many people in Hay who still cannot believe in Armstrong's guilt, and to be fair a jury today would probably decide that the purely circumstantial evidence was insufficient to prove beyond reasonable doubt that he killed his wife. On the balance of probability, when the facts of Mrs Armstrong's medical history are considered, it is quite possible that she took the arsenic herself, either by accident or intent. She had little faith in conventional medicine and none whatever in Tom Hincks. Not only did she doubt his diagnostic capabilities she was also fearful of being returned to the asylum. The nurse was well aware that she was taking her own medicine right up until Monday, 21

February, the day before she died. She regularly left Katharine for half an hour while she had her lunch and occasionally during the afternoon when she took a walk. Sometimes, but by no means on every occasion, the maid, Inez Rosser, was sent to sit with Mrs Armstrong during the nurse's absence. On the morning of 21 February, Nurse Allen left her for at least an hour while she walked to Dr Hincks's surgery to collect some nutrient suppositories. Was it then that Katharine, desperate to get better, took the arsenic that killed her? At Barnwood she had been given a tonic containing arsenic and her condition improved. Had she, perhaps, since her return to Mayfield, been dosing herself with little pinches of arsenic as a tonic? The postmortem findings certainly pointed to repeated small doses in the weeks before her death. Perhaps she felt a larger dose was now required. She knew there was arsenic in the house and where it was kept in the study. Did she come across it on the morning she was taken ill, whilst searching for Sonny's lost book? And did she take some up to her room that day, keeping a secret supply under her pillow or in the medicine chest close to her bed? And did she confuse it with one of her special homeopathic powders? There were, after all, numerous bottles, boxes and sachets crammed into the medicine chest—a confusing array for someone as mentally disturbed as Katharine undoubtedly was at the time.

The idea that she may have stored some of the arsenic in one of her own homeopathic medicine bottles is given credence by her eldest daughter, Eleanor. Though too young to testify at her father's trial, she nevertheless confided in a neighbour, Mary Tunnard Moore, saying; 'When Mummy was so ill she told me to be very careful with the bottles, because if she took the wrong one and anything happened, Daddy would be blamed.'

Or did Katharine, sick, distraught and confused, take a pinch of white arsenic accidentally, mistaking it for bicarbonate of soda, which the nurse had given her when she was billious?

Unfortunately, it is never possible in a case such as this to know what really happened—how this particular tragedy came about, more than seventy years ago. Or explain why, even now, the little Major continues to hold such a particular fascination for criminologists. A man, very much of his time, a true Edwardian, dutiful, resourceful and diligent whose life, by his own admission, centred on his family and work. A man who, until his arrest, had led an unremarkable life, elevated only by the stoicism with which he met his death—an infamous death which may have been brought about, not by the crime of murder at all, but by fate and the ill-concealed malice in other men's hearts.

Fred Davies and Oswald Martin left Hay soon after Armstrong's execution. Martin died in 1946, aged 56. Marion Gale died in 1960, aged 91. Dr Tom Hincks died of a heart attack whilst riding in the fields behind Mayfield, in 1932. He was 57.

The 'poisoned chocolates' were kept by Sir William Willcox and frequently exhibited during his lectures on toxicology at St Mary's Hospital, London.

X

The Butler of Burghill Court

The scene of this unusual case was the village of Burghill, some six miles north west of Hereford. The parish church, St Mary the Virgin, was built in 1275 and, despite a number of subsequent restorations, it has retained the Norman font that so inspired Edward Elgar that he cycled from Hereford to draw it.

In 1926, the occupants of Burghill Court, undoubtedly the most imposing country house in the area, were the Woodhouse sisters, both spinsters—Miss Elinor Drinkwater Woodhouse, known as Miss Ella and aged sixty-five and Miss Martha Gordon Woodhouse, known as Miss May, who was fifty-seven. They were wealthy and, like their mother before them, imperious and dictatorial.

Their father, John George Gordon Woodhouse, a prosperous wine merchant, had bought Burghill House in 1875 and, following the Victorian vogue for pseudo-royal pretensions, changed the name to Burghill Court. The family, mindful of their position in society, soon became involved in the affairs of the village and subscribed to a number of local causes—in particular the fund-raising efforts for the restoration of the ancient parish church.

When Mrs Woodhouse senior died in 1923, Burghill Court was left to their brother, Mr Gordon Woodhouse, but, as he already owned an estate in Yorkshire, he allowed his sisters to remain in the house. Miss Ella and Miss May were well provided for and able to maintain a very comfortable life-style; they employed a coachman, Mr John Towne, who lived with his wife, Fanny, in the Estate Offices, and several men to work on the estate. In addition they had four live-in domestic servants—a cook, Mrs Mary Ann Smith, a house-keeper, two maids and a butler, Charles Houghton. In Edwardian society, retaining the services of an indoor manservant had been considered highly prestigious, the majority of houses making do with cheaper female labour—a cook and one or possibly two maids-of-all-work. Charles Houghton, at forty-five, was a relic of that era—the gentleman's gentleman. He had been with the Woodhouse family for twenty-one years, starting as a footman and working his way up to the prized position of butler. And it certainly was an excellent post. He was trusted, well-liked, and lived in beautiful surroundings, added to which, as his duties were fairly light, he was able to spend most afternoons shooting on the 300 acre estate, for all the world like a country gentleman. For this he borrowed a 12 bore shot-gun from one of his employers' cousins, Mr Ernest William Jackson, a school master from Brighton, who was a frequent visitor to Burghill Court. After an afternoon's sport the butler would always return the gun to its usual place—behind the door in the pantry.

Over the years Houghton had developed a taste for drink, but for a while retained the ability to give the appearance of sobriety. One cannot help feeling, however, that once he had started to drink to excess these two maiden ladies, albeit shrouded in a mist of lavender water and sal volatile, would have been able to smell liquor at twenty paces. Yet, despite his bouts of inebriation, he was a kindly and courteous man. This is certainly how Mr Towne's granddaughter remembers him. At the age of seven, being rather thin, she was sent from her home in London to stay with the coachman and his wife. She remembers the butler as a friendly and amusing companion; so too, does another lady, related to the Woodhouse family, who often stayed at the Court as a child. As she recalls, the servants were obliged to join the sisters for morning prayers in the echoing grand hall—an ordeal for any five year old, having to keep still and quiet for so long. She has a touching memory of the butler keeping her amused during the service by feeding her raisins.

Burghill Court in 1926

By the summer of 1926 the Woodhouse sisters were well aware that Houghton was drinking heavily with his friends in the village and it worried them greatly. He was often missing when required to serve at table or open the front door to visitors—they may have given him a few discreet warnings about his behaviour but when, on 31 August, Houghton served dinner whilst plainly drunk, it was the last straw. The sisters felt that, not only was he setting a bad example to the other employees, drunken behaviour was totally unacceptable in an all-female household. They decided, reluctantly, to sack him although there was talk of transferring him to their brother's estate in Yorkshire.

Distressed at having to do this, and possibly in need of a little moral support, they waited until Sunday, 6 September, when their brother, Gordon, and cousin, Ernest Jackson, and his wife were staying at the Court. In fact, there seems to have been something of a family gathering that weekend, probably connected with Gordon's decision to sell the house to his sisters for a reputed

£60,000. They had arranged to go into Hereford the following day to see their solicitors and sign the documents necessary for the transferal of the deeds. In the circumstances it must have seemed the most opportune moment to dismiss Houghton or arrange his transfer to Yorkshire.

So it was that on Sunday afternoon Houghton was sent for and told by Miss Elinor that, although she did not harbour any anger or ill-feeling towards him, his drinking propensity was such that she and her sister had decided to get rid of him. Houghton made no attempt to deny that he had been drunk during dinner the week before but said that, as the cook had not given him enough to eat, he had sustained himself with liquor. But the ladies dismissed this feeble excuse, refused to reconsider their decision and gave him twenty four hours' notice.

Understandably this came as a great shock and he protested at being given so little time after twenty-one years' service. He was offered a transfer to Yorkshire but rejected the idea of being suddenly uprooted and transplanted, like a piece of furniture, to an estate where he knew no one. After some discussion it was agreed to let him stay until the end of the week; he was also given a month's wages in lieu of notice. Houghton went up to his room, absolutely devastated by what had happened. He even refused to come down and serve dinner that evening. He knew perfectly well that few households in the area could afford a butler, and considering his age and drink problem he knew he was unlikely to find employment elsewhere. After all, he had lived at Burghill Court all his adult life, and had some good friends in the village—it was his home, not just his place of work. The cook, realising how upset he was, felt sorry for him and took some bread and milk up to his room.

The following morning he seemed to have adjusted to his forth-coming dismissal. He came down, had his breakfast in the servants' hall and at 8.45 a.m. attended morning prayers with the rest of the household. His behaviour seemed perfectly normal. The day's routine proceeded as usual; he served breakfast to the sisters without making any reference to his dismissal; everyone thought he was taking it very well indeed in the circumstances.

Soon after 9.30 Houghton appeared in the kitchen with some coffee in a silver pot for Mary Smith, the cook. She said later that he seemed 'just the same as always'. Mary asked when Miss Elinor Woodhouse would be coming down to discuss the day's arrangements and the butler replied; 'She will be round in a minute' and left the room. A few minutes later, at 9.45, Miss Elinor came into the kitchen and spent about ten minutes talking to the cook. Then, as she went back through the kitchen door into the passage, she was shot at point blank range. A second shot followed almost immediately accompanied by dreadful screams. Probably without thinking the cook opened the kitchen door to see what had happened and heard someone running up the back stairs to the butler's bedroom.

At the same moment she saw the body of Miss Elinor slumped in the passage close to the kitchen door, with a gunshot wound close to her neck. Further along the passage, near the back stair lobby, she saw Miss May 'unconscious and bleeding profusely'. At the same time, the housemaid, Beatrice Cotterell, had heard the two shots from the top of the back stairs and, thinking Houghton had shot himself, she ran to his room but found the door locked.

Another maid, on her way up the stairs to find the housekeeper, saw Ernest Jackson come out of the smoke room. He said later that he'd heard the first shot and thought it was a tray crashing to the floor—but, recognising the second shot, opened his door just in time to see Houghton disappear into his bedroom. Jackson hurried downstairs and, seeing Miss Elinor's body in the passage, ran out of the front door to summon help. He found the coachman, John Towne, in the stable preparing the pony and trap ready to drive the sisters into Hereford. Towne hurried into the house and found May's body in the lobby. She, too, had been shot at close range and was barely alive. While the coachman cradled Miss May in his arms until she died, Jackson went in search of the weapon. He found his 12 bore shot gun in its usual place behind the pantry door; inside were two spent cartridges.

The police and a doctor were called and arrived at approximately 10.20. Dr Vincent Shaw confirmed that both Miss Elinor and Miss May were dead. Ernest Jackson spoke briefly with Superintendent Albert Weaver* and gave him the shot gun. Weaver, who had known Houghton for some time, went straight upstairs to his room but found it locked. He called out for Houghton to open the door; after a moment or two the door opened a little but when the butler saw Weaver he quickly locked it again. Weaver repeated his order to open up and when he did, managed to grab Houghton's wrist. It was then that he noticed that the butler was bleeding from several lacerations where he had attempted to cut his own throat. Weaver took him down to the storeroom and held on to him while Dr Shaw attended to the wounds; there were seven in number but they were fairly superficial. At this point, Houghton said to Weaver: 'Oh, dear! This is a bad job, Super.' The policeman agreed, to which the butler replied: 'It is passion.'

Before leaving the house, Weaver searched Houghton and found two unfired cartridges; he then took him straight to Hereford County Police Station, his neck swathed in bandages. When charged with the murder of the Woodhouse sisters he said: 'I do not wish to say anything.'

When asked if he wanted to attend the inquest into the ladies' death he declined, saying, 'I do not wish to attend. I cannot do any good.'

A week later Charles Houghton was brought from Gloucester Prison to attend the committal proceedings at the magistrates' court in Hereford. A crowd, mainly consisting of women, had already gathered outside the court. The two Woodhouse sisters were well-known in the area for their support of many worthy causes and it was not surprising that the public gallery was filled with spectators, curious to see the man accused of their murder. Houghton was given the opportunity to have a solicitor defend him but, having no money, he declined. He appeared before the Bench in a light raincoat over the same navy blue suit he was wearing on the day of his arrest, and his neck was still bandaged.

* In 1922, when he was Deputy Chief Constable of Herefordshire, he had assisted Chief Inspector Crutchett, of New Scotland Yard, to arrest Major Armstrong at Hay.

Mr G.R. Paling, outlined the case on behalf of the Director of Public Prosecutions, and called Ernest Jackson, Mary Smith, the cook, and the maid, Beatrice Cotterell, as witnesses. Weaver told of Houghton's arrest and the finding of the shot gun and the two spent cartridges. Dr Shaw testified that both ladies had been shot at close range and confirmed that whereas Miss Elinor had died instantly, Miss May had remained alive but unconscious for several minutes.

When formally charged with the murders and asked if he had anything to say Houghton replied: 'No, sir.' When asked what means he had to pay for a counsel to defend him he said: 'Not a great deal, sir.'

When it was ascertained that he had less than £7 to his name he was granted a certificate, (legal aid), to pay for his defence. According to a reporter in *The Hereford Times* he 'remained in Court some time after the general public had left, and chatted for several minutes with Commander Drinkwater, a cousin of the deceased ladies. The accused also had a conversation with his brother, his stepbrother, and friends, and also the cook and Miss Cotterell. He appeared in good spirits, and smiled occasionally. He was later taken to the County Police Station through a side exit and returned to Gloucester (gaol) late in the afternoon.'

More than a thousand mourners attended the sisters' funeral. It was described as a 'simple and beautiful' occasion when 'every resident in the district, from the oldest to the youngest, and from the richest to the poorest, seemed to be present.' The gardeners and outdoor staff conveyed the two coffins, which were laid on wheeled biers, from the house to the church of St Mary the Virgin. According to *The Hereford Times*:

'Slowly and sadly the procession wend its way from the scene of the tragedy through the avenue of overhanging boughs, footed by a bed of beautiful flowers and then along the long drive by the side of which the tall trees rustled a mournful adieu out on to the main road lined by sorrowing cottagers.

'Behind the biers walked Mr J.G. Gordon Woodhouse, the sole surviving immediate relative, with other private mourners, and in turn came members of the household staff, each dressed in deep mourning and carrying a huge wreath of lovely flowers. At the rear of the funeral cortege was the deceased ladies' favourite pony, drawing a carriage full of floral tributes, and a motor car similarly laden.

'A midsummerlike sun shone as the procession steadily climbed the hill of mourning to the church, the silence being now and again broken by the tolling of the bell and the sobbing of women and children among the spectators who lined the route. Then through the shade of the friendly yew trees it passed into the mellow light of the church, wherein are tablets perpetuating the noble lives of the deceaseds' parents and visible signs of their own love and generosity.'

The service ended with the 'ethereal, pulsating and, finally, triumphant strains of the Dead March. The Woodhouse sisters' graves—the bricked sides white-washed and surmounted with a wide black border—were decorated with brightly coloured dahlias, their favourite flowers.' Close by were their parents' graves and in another lay the body of an old retainer, Ellen George, who had served the Woodhouse family for thirty-six years.

After the three officiating vicars and chief mourners—among them the staff and pupils of two local schools and representatives of various charitable associations—had gone back to the church 'the villagers filed past the grave casting loving and sorrowing eyes on where their "ladies bountiful" slept. Most pathetic of all was the way in which the oldest of the employees lingered by the graveside, weeping unrestrainedly because of the sadness within them. From the church floated the solemn strains of the organ, heavy with grief but expressing in music "thoughts which lay too deep for tears". When the sun went down the ladies were left alone with the flowers that so fittingly symbolised the beauty and saintliness of their lives.'

Two months later equally vast crowds had gathered outside the Shire Hall, Hereford, on the morning of Friday, 7 November, for the trial of Charles Houghton. He was brought from

Gloucester Prison by train, as Major Armstrong had been four years before. The case came before Mr Justice Rigby Swift with Mr Ronald Powell for the prosecution and Mr A.J. Long for the defence—instructed by the Hereford solicitor, Mr F. Craze. Charged first with the murder of Miss Elinor Woodhouse and then with that of Miss May Woodhouse, Houghton replied firmly and in a clear voice: 'Not Guilty'.

Outlining the background of the case for the jury Mr Powell said that 'by reason of their social position and the length of time they [the sisters] had been in the neighbourhood they were well known to all in the district and were looked upon with great respect and great affection by all who knew them.'

He went on to describe Charles Houghton's place in the household as being a 'very comfortable billet', one which he had every reason to expect to enjoy for the rest of his working life. During the summer the prisoner had become 'intemperate in his habits' and, as he was the only man living in a household of women, the sisters felt it best that he should go. He went on to describe the events that followed the butler's dismissal and the tragic shooting the following day.

Ernest Jackson was called as a witness and testified that the relationship between the Misses Woodhouse and their staff had always been 'of the happiest character'—in the circumstances, he did not doubt for one moment that the prisoner was greatly upset by his dismissal.

When the cook, Mrs Mary Ann Smith*, took the stand she admitted that she had noticed that Houghton had been drinking heavily throughout the summer. Questioned by the defence, Mrs Smith confirmed that the butler had previously been a 'hard-working, faithful servant'. She testified that he valued his position very highly and was very distressed at being sacked. He told her it was a disgrace that he was given such short notice and felt the only solution was to 'end it himself'.

---

* According to Mrs Smith's grandson, Fred Bond, Mary was so traumatised by the murders that she suffered badly with her nerves thereafter and, for a while, experienced some paralysis down her left side.

Miss Beatrice Cotterell, the second housemaid, then told the court her version of the events. She was followed into the witness box by Dr Vincent Shaw, who, again questioned by the defence, admitted that although Houghton was on his panel of patients he had never treated him—nor did he realise, as it was now suggested, that he suffered from epilepsy. He confirmed that a person with epilepsy might go for years between attacks and appear to be in excellent health. Although he conceded that it was, in theory, possible that Houghton had shot the two ladies as a result of an epileptic seizure, he thought it unlikely as, when he examined him about half an hour later, he seemed perfectly normal.

This evidence was endorsed by Weaver who said that he knew Houghton well and had never known him have an attack of epilepsy. When he saw him shortly after the murders he seemed 'remarkably cool under the circumstances'.

Charles Houghton's sister, Mrs Sarah Worrall, was called for the defence. She confirmed that her brother, who had lived at home until the age of fourteen, had suffered childhood convulsions on three occasions—he had, she said, 'lain on his bed, clenched his hands, foamed at the mouth, and gone black in the face'.

A specialist on epilepsy, Dr C. Francis, was called and explained to the court that he had examined Charles Houghton earlier that day and found 'his intellect dull and he seemed to take a very casual interest in the examination'. He also found that his right ear drum had been ruptured causing a 'chronic suppurative inflammation.' On close questioning Houghton admitted to having received a blow to the head 'some time ago'. Examination of his knee and wrist jerks, along with other features, made the doctor consider the possibility of the presence of 'some cerebral irritation.' He went further to say that he thought it quite possible that Houghton's childhood convulsions were epileptic in origin and, moreover, the shock and worry of his sudden dismissal might well have brought on an epileptic attack. As to the possibility of Houghton, if he was in the throes of an attack, being able to carry out the murders, the doctor said that 'it is wellknown that an [untreated] epileptic may do something in an organised manner although he has no knowledge of it himself'.*

The last witness to be called was Dr Bell, the medical officer at Gloucester Prison, who said that, whilst in custody, Charles Houghton had 'showed no signs of insanity or epilepsy or mental disease'.

The case against Charles Houghton, though circumstantial in that no one actually saw him fire the gun at the two ladies, was a most convincing one. But it remained for the prosecution to persuade the jury that Houghton, according to M'Naughton's Law,* knew what he was doing when he aimed the gun and pulled the trigger, and, moreover, he knew that what he was doing was wrong. Since the M'Naughton case in 1843, the law stipulated that a person could not be convicted if proved insane— if, that is, when the crime was committed, that person firstly, did not know what they were doing and secondly, was incapable of distinguishing right from wrong—that person was deemed not responsible for their actions.

---

* Epilepsy has been used as a defence in a number of murder cases. Lee Harvey Oswald, the alleged killer of President John F. Kennedy in 1963, was himself shot by Jack Ruby. At his subsequent trial he pleaded 'Not Guilty' on the grounds that he was undergoing a psychomotor seizure at the time of the shooting. According to a number of expert witnesses, including Dr Roy Schaffer, a clinical psychologist at Yale University, sufferers of this disorder are prone to uncontrollable and explosive behaviour if emotionally upset—their consciousness is impaired and aggressive acts may be committed automatically. Other experts, however, did not agree that this was the case when Ruby shot Oswald. He was found guilty and sentenced to death, but died in custody of cancer in 1967.

A survey conducted by specialists at the Maudesley Hospital in 1953 found that of 105 murderers screened, 18 showed symptoms of epilepsy, some thirty times greater than the incidence of the disorder among the general population.

* M'Naughten was a young artisan with a persecution complex and was convinced he was being spied upon by Sir Robert Peel. In 1843, he shot Peel's private secretary by mistake; as a result of his trial and the verdict of 'Insanity' the M'Naughten Rules were introduced to safeguard those who kill whilst suffering from mental illness.

The jury at Charles Houghton's trial was clearly convinced that he was perfectly sane at the time of the murders, knew what he was doing and that it was wrong, and dismissed the defence proposition that he was suffering from an epileptic seizure at the time. They brought a verdict of guilty on both counts and Mr Justice Rigby Swift sentenced the prisoner to death.

Mr Craze, Houghton's solicitor, in the ten days allowed after conviction, put up a gallant fight on his client's behalf. He submitted various documents relating to evidence that Charles Houghton suffered a number of epileptic attacks whilst serving as a soldier in the First World War. These were lodged with the Court of Criminal Appeal and in consequence of this the arrangements for Houghton's execution at Gloucester Prison on 23 November were suspended until the outcome of the appeal.

But a week later, after consultation with the Home Secretary, who 'decided he was unable to intervene', the appeal failed. Charles Houghton's execution was set for eight o'clock on the morning of 4 December, 1926. But whereas on the morning of Major Armstrong's execution four years earlier a crowd of more than two thousand had gathered outside the prison gates since dawn, there was little interest in Charles Houghton. A reporter noted that 'half an hour before the execution there was hardly a soul to be seen in the dim greyness of the cold morning. From time to time business people on their way to work paused to glance at the customary notice posted on the prison door overnight' prior to the execution.

The state executioner, Thomas Pierrepoint, and his assistant had, in accordance with the regulations, arrived the day before to spend the night in the prison. Various officials arrived early the next day—the Vicar of St Mary de Lode, in which parish the prison stood, the Under-Sheriff of Herefordshire and the prison doctor. As it neared eight o'clock a small group of women congregated near the door of the prison and watched the arrival of the prison Governor, Mr Whyte. *The Hereford Times* described the scene as follows:

'A few minutes before eight o'clock the bell of St Mary de Lode commenced to toll and was still tolling as the hour struck.

146

Amid the noise of the adjacent works, the bustle of the lorries in the square, and a postman delivering letters at the Gaol almost at the moment of execution, there was nothing beyond the gathering of the small crowd to indicate that anything unusual was passing within.

'Charles Houghton, dressed in a navy blue suit, which he wore at the trial, was visited by the Chaplain on the latter's arrival. A few minutes before eight o'clock Pierrepoint and his assistant entered the condemned cell and expeditiously carried out the pinioning. Immediately the folding door separating the cell from the execution chamber was thrown open, and just a few steps took the condemned man on to the scaffold. Within a few seconds of his leaving the cell he had expiated his crime in the presence of the Under Sheriff of Herefordshire, the Governor, the prison doctor, the Chaplain, and one or two warders. The warders leaving a few minutes past the hour was an indication that Houghton had paid the extreme penalty, for it is customary to disallow anyone to enter or leave the prison about the time of execution.'

The small crowd remained outside the gates to witness the posting of two notices, one confirming that the execution had been carried out and the other, signed by the prison doctor, to confirm that Charles Houghton was now dead. A few remained to watch the departure of the officials a few minutes later.

To comply with the law an inquest on Houghton's death was carried out within the precincts of the prison before the coroner for North Gloucestershire, Mr James Waghorne, a jury of nine, the prison Governor, a doctor and three reporters. The jury were obliged to view the body and confirm that it was that of Charles Houghton. The Governor then stated that the execution was carried out 'expeditiously'. The doctor also confirmed that death was 'absolutely instantaneous' caused by 'the dislocation of the neck.'

Thanking the jurors for their attendance, the Coroner was at pains to stress that both Charles Houghton and Major Armstrong had committed their crimes in adjoining Herefordshire, not Gloucestershire—and the fact that they were executed in

Gloucestershire was not a reflection on the criminality of that county but simply 'owing to the closing of the county prisons of Worcestershire and Herefordshire'.

Which, in the circumstances, was rather a heartlessly dismissive remark to make in view of the tragic events that had led to the death of three women and two men.

XI

The Tragic Widow of Coleford

When thirty-six year old sheep farmer and quarryman, Harry Pace, died on 10 January, 1928, most people assumed that arsenic in the sheep dip was responsible. Although he earned little as a quarryman he had managed to acquire a flock of eighty sheep, which had become the ruling passion in his life—it was said that he thought of little else. At his farm in the Forest of Dean in July the previous year he had, with the help of his wife, Beatrice, spent some eight hours dipping his precious flock. Shortly afterwards he had fallen ill—he began to vomit violently and complained of acute abdominal pain. A little later, having developed paralysis in his arms and legs, he was admitted to Gloucester Infirmary where he was treated over a period of three months for peripheral neuritis caused, as it was thought, by the arsenic in the sheep dip.

During his stay in hospital Beatrice Pace had visited often and, according to a number of witnesses, showed great concern for her husband and seemed anxious for his ultimate recovery. So much so, in fact, that the nurses found her a 'positive nuisance'. In October 1927 he was allowed home although both the doctors and Beatrice felt he was not fully recovered and should have stayed in hospital a little longer. On his return he made some progress but just before Christmas he had a relapse, suffering once more from acute abdominal pain, vomiting and paralysis in his limbs. He died in great agony on 10 January.

However, certain members of the Pace family, his brother, Elton, in particular, were not so sure that the sheep dip was to blame. There was talk of deliberate poisoning and the day after Harry died Elton 'made certain representations' to the county coroner, Mr Maurice Carter. The effect was dramatic. The coroner sent an officer to stop the funeral and informed the police authorities, who immediately drafted in extra help in the form of two officers from Scotland Yard. The coroner then ordered a postmortem examination, an operation was performed by Dr Carson of Lydney, who sent various organs taken from the body for further examination by a pathologist at Bristol University.

The results of the analysis were such that the coroner ordered an inquest into the death of Harry Pace. It was held in Coleford on 17 January but was immediately adjourned to allow the police more time for their investigations. The inquest was reopened on 12 April, and Harry's brother, Elton, was called to give evidence. He told the coroner that his sister-in-law, Beatrice, thought he was a bully and wouldn't let him in the house. He went on to say that he'd often heard her declare that she wished her husband was dead and once said that she would 'poison the bastard'. Asked what had brought about such a vindictive remark, Elton Pace said that she had been picking fault with her husband's 'ways, and his meanness, and said she wished she was single'. On one occasion, he confided, she had even intimated that she had someone else in mind to replace him. Asked by Mr Trevor Wellington, the solicitor acting for Mrs Pace, whether he had ever made any 'improper overtures' to his client, his reply was adamant: 'My God! no. You be careful what you are saying.'

He then went on to insinuate that a certain married man, a Mr Sayce, frequently called on Mrs Pace while her husband was out. There followed an angry exchange between Wellington and Pace during which a lewd comment, unprintable in the papers of the day, was made that caused such laughter from the spectators that a police officer warned all present that the court was not a theatre, the case in hand was 'a very serious one' and he would ask them all to leave if there was any further outbreaks of laughter.

During the course of his questioning, Elton Pace denied that he had ever suggested that one of Beatrice's gentleman friends, Mr Sayce, had poisoned Harry. Nor had he called out 'Armstrong' as he followed him down the road,* or mentioned him in particular when he contacted the coroner with his suspicions.

Further insinuations about Beatrice's alleged immorality came from Harry Pace's sister, Mrs Leah Pritchard, who told the court that on one occasion she had made a surprise visit to the Paces' home during Harry's absence and Beatrice had come downstairs with her hair and clothing dishevelled. One can imagine the nods and knowing looks that passed between the spectators gathered in the public gallery as they listened to such scandalous revelations. It must have been clear to Beatrice, her solicitor and the coroner's jury, that allegations such as these were intended to depict a far from happy marriage—with the obvious inference that she might have wished to rid herself of the husband she had already betrayed. It was, undeniably, evidence that could incriminate her, and although she was not without support from a small band of friends, she looked decidedly anxious. As she entered the court after the interval for lunch a woman in the crowd called out: 'Keep your heart up. God be with you.'

Despite this attempt to boost her spirits Beatrice began to cry during the afternoon's proceedings and, noticing that she was swaying in her seat, a police woman propped her up, gave her a sip of water and liberally applied the smelling salts.

The proceedings were resumed on Wednesday 18 April, and Harry's sister, Gertrude Pace, continued to cast aspersions on Beatrice's moral behaviour by declaring that she hadn't visited Beatrice for two years as she 'didn't like her ways'. She, too, testified to hearing Beatrice say she would 'poison the old bastard' and went on to insinuate that her sister-in-law entertained, not only Mr Sayce, but also a Mr Harold Cole, for tea.

That same day Beatrice's daughter, seventeen year old Dorothy, was called to give evidence. She had been in service at the Red Lion Inn, Hereford, when her father had been hospitalised in Gloucester. When she returned to the family home in November she found her father ill in bed. In the course of her

---

* The case of Major Armstrong had excited interest on a national scale six years before—and, in some people's minds, his name had become synonymous with poison.

151

testimony she admitted that her father had 'a violent temper at times' and had often mistreated her mother, herself and all the children.

When questioned further on this point Dorothy seemed reluctant to elaborate but did say, after a long pause: 'He was never very kind to me. He would get into fits of temper and lock us out, children and all.'

A little later she added: 'I remember father beating mother at the bottom of the stairs. Once, about a year ago, he got a walking stick and beat mother across the back.'

Dorothy also said that she had heard her father talk of suicide many times and a week after Christmas he'd said he wished he could get something 'to finish himself off'. It was apparent to everyone in court that the girl had both feared and disliked her father and when asked by the coroner if she had 'any regard, any feeling, or any love' for him, she paused for a long time before replying in a quiet voice: 'To father? No, sir.'

Further questioning established that Dorothy had gone upstairs on Christmas Day to light a fire in her father's room; he told her not to bother as he would be coming downstairs. As the girl put the kindling into the fender she noticed a bottle there. She put it on the chest of drawers before going back downstairs to tell her mother. It was left to subsequent witnesses to describe what happened later that day.

The following day a Mr Reginald Martin was called to give evidence. He stated that he was a grocer and confectioner and he had visited Harry Pace every Sunday morning since his release from hospital in October. When he saw him on the Sunday before he died Harry was looking very ill and told Martin that he'd strained himself going down to join the family on Christmas Day and had a pain across his abdomen. The grocer went on to describe what had happened that day. At a quarter past twelve the Paces' youngest daughter, Doris, in a highly nervous state, had run to fetch him saying that her father 'had got a razor and was going to kill them all'. When Reginald Martin reached the house he found Harry Pace, not in a temper at all but 'quiet, calm and collected' and persuaded him to go back upstairs to bed. He was not surprised, however, to find that he had calmed down so quickly for, he told the coroner, Harry Pace was a very peculiar man. 'His chief object in life seemed to be his sheep and he made no reference to anything else.'

When Martin arrived on Christmas Day Dorothy had whispered to him that she had found a green bottle marked 'Poison' in the fender and thought her father may 'have taken something'. He concluded by saying that Harry had never complained about the way his wife was looking after him and seemed perfectly satisfied with his treatment.

Next came a series of witnesses who had been fellow patients of Harry Pace at the Gloucester Infirmary. The first was a collier, Charles Alfred Fletcher. He had visited Harry after his discharge and said that Harry had told him that whenever he took his medicine 'everything went black and he was in agony with pain in his stomach'. Whereupon he had taken a sip of Pace's medicine and assured him that 'there was not much taste attached to it' and suggested that he take more water with it. In answer to further questioning by Beatrice's solicitor, Mr Wellington, Fletcher said that when he told Beatrice about the medicine causing her husband pain she was 'distressed and went to the doctor's about it'.

Another friend who visited Harry Pace after he left hospital was Fred Thorne, a miner. As he had some experience as a masseur, Harry's mother had asked him to massage his legs. This he did every day except Sundays and, in his opinion, Pace was making some progress, until, just before Christmas his condition deteriorated; he began to vomit and was in great pain. When Fletcher saw him the day before he died Pace had said: 'I am suffering hell. I wish something would happen one way or the other.' He said he had an awful thumping in his head and his heart was 'beating terribly'.

Another of Harry Pace's fellow patients was Arthur Ernest Smith. He told the jury that Pace had been so severely depressed that he had often burst into tears and on a couple of occasions said that if he didn't get any better he would 'do himself in'. Smith confirmed that Beatrice Pace had visited her husband regularly, twice a week, bringing sweets, fruit and cakes—which the witness gladly helped him eat—and he had never heard him speak ill of his wife.

Next to take the stand was Edwin Percy Morgan, who worked for a colliery and was also an ex-patient at Gloucester Infirmary. He told the coroner that Pace was 'always very despondent and would break into tears for long periods, this happening on numerous occasions'. He appeared to have readily accepted that his illness was caused by arsenic in the sheep dip but could not reconcile himself to the thought of his legs being permanently paralysed.

Inspector Bent, from the local constabulary, was called next; he described the various visits to Mrs Pace he and Sergeant Hambling had made after the coroner had received 'certain representations' from Elton Pace. Beatrice readily handed over a packet of sheep dip of the type her husband had used and one or two bottles—one of which was the small green bottle found in the fender. He went on to describe his visit to the chemist shop in Coleford where he checked the Sale of Poisons Register; this confirmed that two packets of sheep dip had been sold to Harry Pace on 22 July, 1927, the register signed by Mrs Pace.

It was not until 5 March that the police were officially informed that Harry Pace had died of arsenical poisoning. On one of several visits to Beatrice he explained that the Scotland Yard detectives wished to interview her. She readily agreed to go into Coleford Police Station and later that afternoon a search was made of the house. Various bottles were sent to the county analyst of Gloucester.

It was at this point in the proceedings that Beatrice Pace's statement to the police was read out in court. It was a depressing document, a catalogue of domestic violence and suffering:

'We were married when I was 17 years of age. The marriage has been most unhappy in consequence of my husband being of a jealous nature and his cruelty. The first day we were married he started to beat me in his temper and he beat me occasionally the whole of my married life until he was taken ill. The last time he beat me was before my baby was born when he thrashed me with a walking stick.

Mrs Pace

'In Ellwood, he beat me with a piece of wire rope and I ran
home to my father's house in St Briavels. At two o'clock in the
morning my husband came to the house and shouted: "Tell her to
put her head out of the window and she will get the contents of
this". He had a gun in his hand. He used to swear at me and
called me vile things, and this also caused unhappiness between

us. In the early part of last year my husband assaulted me with a strap and I reported this to Sergeant Hambling and he saw my husband.

'I also summoned him on one occasion several years ago for knocking me about and he was bound over to be of good behaviour. There is no truth in rumours that men have come to see me for immoral purposes. Mr Leslie Sayce, of Ellwood, who was a friend of my husband, came to our house occasionally and he used to look after the sheep. Another man has also been to the house to do odd jobs for my husband. Certainly intimacy never took place between us. Mrs Sayce has been to my house with her husband on many occasions and she could prove there was nothing wrong between us.'

The statement continued with Mrs Pace saying her husband was 'a very lustful man' who had twice been in trouble for indecently assaulting girls. She went on to say that her husband was 'careless with his dip leaving it in the tub for days'. She further stated that 'when a lamb of ours got onto the railway line and was killed he went into a temper and took hold of my Pomeranian dog and knocked its brains out against the wall. On Christmas day he came down and sat by the fire. He suddenly took up the tongs and said; "I will knock your f...... brains out." My daughter shielded me and then he took a razor out of the cupboard and told us to clear out, all of us. I sent for Mr Martin and then my husband became calm. He went upstairs and cried continually from dinner-time till tea-time. This was the last time he came downstairs.'

Before the policeman left the witness box he was questioned closely by Trevor Wellington and virtually admitted that Elton Pace had, in his initial representation to the coroner, suggested that Mr Sayce had 'administered poison and was guilty of immoral conduct'.

The next witness to take the stand was Beatrice's neighbour, Mrs Rosa Kear, who said that Harry Pace had been taken ill during the sheep dipping and a girl who had seen him writhing on the ground in pain, had laughed, thinking he was drunk. She told the court that she had been with Beatrice and Mrs Sayce when

Harry had died and, contrary to what Mrs Pritchard had said, he had died, not in 'agonising pain' but 'peacefully.'

At this point the proceedings were adjourned once more; when the enquiry reopened Beatrice Pace was once more in attendance. A reporter described her as a 'pathetic figure' constantly dabbing her eyes with her handkerchief as she listened to the evidence concerning the financial value of her husband's sheep and the debts still to be paid. Her friend, Mrs Alice May Sayce, was called and agreed that Mrs Pritchard's lies about being at her brother's death bed were as 'perfect nonsense' as were the rumours that her husband, Leslie Sayce, was having an affair with Beatrice Pace.

The gentleman in question, Leslie Sayce, was then called to take the stand and told the coroner that as far as he was concerned the rumour connecting him with Mrs Pace was malicious gossip started by the Pace family, Mrs Pritchard in particular. As a constant visitor to the Pace household he knew of the unhappy marriage and as a family friend, little Doris had told him that she didn't get any dinner on Christmas Day because her 'daddy had got up and caused a bother, smashing the fireguard up with the tongs and the trouble prevented the dinner being made ready'.

In answer to questions put to him by Trevor Wellington, Sayce admitted that he and Elton Pace had recently quarrelled; he said that Pace had accused him of poisoning his brother and called him 'Armstrong'. 'He also accused me of immoral relations with his sister-in-law. I reported it to Inspector Bent and I and my wife went to see you, (Mr Wellington). Elton Pace was warned and in consequence he has since kept a quiet tongue in his head.'

All these rumours and allegations must have been extremely distressing for Beatrice Pace. It was even worse when she had to watch her nine year old son, Leslie, take the stand. When he was asked by the coroner if he was happy at home he replied: 'No. On Christmas Day dad got a razor and said he was going to cut our throats.' He also remembered the time his father had threatened to shoot them all. But, he added, his mother was kind to him and he was very fond of her.

Young Leslie was followed into the box by his sister, Dorothy, recalled for questioning by the coroner. She admitted that while she was away in service she had purchased two-penny worth of salts of lemon to clean her work apron and had posted them home in readiness for the weekend. She had mixed the salts in a saucer and afterwards threw the remainder away. The two policemen from Scotland Yard, however, had pestered and harassed her into saying that she had poured the mixture into a bottle, insinuating that it was this fluid that had caused her father's death. In the end, she said, she 'let them go with it and I said I put it in the bottle to shut their mouths up.' They also repeatedly called her a liar and suggested that she and her mother had poisoned her father.*

Leaving this disturbing testimony in abeyance the coroner adjourned the enquiry, it being seven o'clock in the evening.

The enquiry was resumed six days later, on 9 May, nearly four months after Harry Pace's death, with the ominous presence of Mr G.R. Paling, a solicitor with the Director of Prosecutions, appointed to examine the witnesses on behalf of the Home Office.* He was accompanied by the Chief Constable of Gloucester, the Chief Superintendent from the Cheltenham force, and two officers from Scotland Yard. Their presence emphasised the way the enquiry was leading. The sight of them arriving in court that day must have terrified Beatrice Pace, already frightened and distraught by such a long and revealing enquiry.

The first witness to be called was Dr Dupré who had treated Harry Pace throughout his illness. He described in some detail his patient's various symptoms and it became clear that Beatrice Pace had enlisted the doctor's help on a number of occasions—at least three times in the week prior to his death. She had done everything she could to relieve her husband's pain. But on the morning of 10 January Harry Pace was dead; the death certificate,

---

* On Wednesday 23 May, a question was raised in the House of Commons concerning the 'third degree' methods used by the Scotland Yard detectives during the interrogation of Beatrice Pace and two of her children. They were allegedly kept without food or drink for thirteen hours. Mrs Pace, however, publicly complimented the police on the way she had been treated.
* Mr Paling appeared for the Crown in both the Armstrong case of 1922, and the Charles Houghton case of 1926.

signed by Dr Dupré, stated that death was caused by influenza, anuria, gastro-enteritis and peripheral neuritis. Asked by Mr Paling what the witness *now* considered to have been the cause of death he replied 'poisoning by arsenic' at the same time emphasising that none of the medication given to Pace during his illness contained any arsenic whatsoever.

Dr C. Carson, who performed the postmortem on Pace's body also gave the opinion that death was due to arsenical poisoning. Further medical evidence was given the following day by Mr Roland Oliver Ellis, public analyst for Gloucestershire; he estimated that 9.12 grains of arsenic were found in the body's organs, a minimum of two grains being considered a potentially fatal dose. When he began to give details of his analysis the effect on Beatrice Pace was such that she collapsed and 'had to be assisted from the court to which she did not return' that day. There followed lengthy descriptions of the various solutions found in bottles taken from the Pace home—at the end of the day the jury was left in no doubt that the medical experts were of the opinion that Harry Pace had died from a large dose of arsenic taken shortly before his death. As the analyst stepped down from the witness box the enquiry was adjourned yet again.

The afternoon of 15 May was one of tremendous strain for Beatrice Pace as she was called to give evidence. According to the reporter for *The Hereford Times* she 'took the oath composedly and answered questions firmly and without hesitation. Only after she had been in the witness box for three hours did she break down.' Questioned at some length by her solicitor, Trevor Wellington, he finally asked her directly if she had ever, at any time, given poison to her husband. There was a tense silence then Mrs Pace replied in an almost toneless voice: 'No, sir, I did not.' She paused for a fraction of a second and then repeated: 'No, sir, I did not.' She went on to tell the court that her husband had tried to harm himself on a number of occasions. Once he had tried to throw himself from a window but she had managed to pull him back. Asked how she thought her husband had managed to get 9 grains of arsenic in his body she replied: 'I cannot tell you. I cannot tell you.'

As she left the court that day she told a reporter: 'It has been a dreadful ordeal, but I could not have rested without going into the witness-box.'

It had apparently also been something of an ordeal for her solicitor, Trevor Wellington, for he collapsed in court and had to be replaced by Dr W.G. Earengey. Professor Isaac Walker Hall, pathologist at Bristol University, began the proceedings by describing the postmortem examination of Harry Pace's body; his widow, already dubbed by the press 'the tragic widow of Coleford', found the subject too distressing, and once again, left the court in tears. The professor was of the opinion that death was due to arsenical poison but disagreed with Ellis that it was necessarily caused by a large dose in the 48 hours before death. He had found extensive damage to Pace's stomach, bowels, liver, heart and kidney and as it was also present in his skin and bone, this indicated a case of long term poisoning as opposed to one large and fatal dose. There was no evidence to show that Pace had been a 'habitual arsenic eater'.* Finally, he was adamant that Pace could not have absorbed such quantities of arsenic through his sheep dipping activities.

Sir William Willcox, a highly respected authority on arsenical poisoning, was called next to give his opinion. He, too, declined to believe that Pace could have absorbed such a quantity of arsenic through seepage of arsenic into his skin; he suggested that the last dose of arsenic must have been taken or administered between six and forty-eight hours before death. He had rarely come across such large amounts of deposited arsenic but mentioned that similar amounts were recorded in the Armstrong case—and, in the Madeleine Smith 'suicide' a colossal 82 grains were found.*

---

* It was proved in the Florence Maybrick trial of 1889 that her husband, James, had been such an habitual arsenic eater, consuming the poison as a restorative. However, Mrs Maybrick was found guilty of poisoning her husband and sentenced to death; she was granted a reprieve and served 15 years in prison.

* Smith was tried for the murder of her lover, Emile L'Angelier in 1857. The jury returned a verdict of 'Not Proven' and she was freed. That L'Angelier committed suicide was also not proved.

On Tuesday, 22 May, the inquest jury heard further medical evidence from the county analyst regarding the amount of arsenic and sulphur found in sheep dip. Mrs Pace, seated in her usual place and partially hidden from public view, chatted quite cheerfully with a relative who had accompanied her. After listening to the coroner's lengthy summing up the courtroom was cleared, leaving the jurors to reach their conclusion.

Fifty-five minutes later they returned the following verdict: 'We find the deceased, Harry Pace, met his death at Fetter Hill on January 10th by arsenical poisoning, administered by some person or persons other than himself. We are agreed that the case calls for further investigations.'

The Coroner, however, was not satisfied with this verdict; he immediately took the extraordinary step of instructing the jury to return a verdict naming the person they felt was responsible for Pace's death. The jurors at first expressed their disagreement but finally, a little over an hour later, they returned a second, more explicit, verdict ending with the words 'administered by Beatrice Annie Pace.'*

On hearing the amended verdict, Mrs Pace cried: 'No, I didn't!' This was accompanied by cries of 'terrible' and 'shame' from her supporters in the public gallery. At this point she collapsed and was led from the room by a policewoman.

That same afternoon, when she had recovered her composure, Beatrice Pace was brought before the Magistrates and formally charged with the murder of her husband. It was reported that 'she went forward to take up her usual position behind the screen which had saved her from the public gaze previously, and almost collapsed again as she was guided instead to the dock. Sinking onto a chair she buried her face in her handkerchief and wept hysterically. She again broke down as the charge of murdering her husband between July 25th 1927 and January 10th 1928 was read over to her.' Before being taken away to Cardiff Prison she

---

* As a result of the Beatrice Pace case an Act of Parliament was passed which limits the duty of the coroner to establishing the cause of death and debars him from naming a specific individual as being responsible.

said: 'I know nothing about it. I am quite innocent. I cannot say anything else.'

Two days later Beatrice was brought from Cardiff to appear in the magistrates' court once more. An eye-witness described her arrival in a 'closed motor car, accompanied by a prison nurse, a wardress, and a warder'. Mr Paling, conducting the proceedings on behalf of the Director of Public Prosecutions, was flanked by the two Scotland Yard officers. According to the reporter from *The Hereford Times*:

'Mrs Pace, who was less composed than on her previous appearance was given a seat at the end of of the small dock, her chair being positioned in a doorway against the sides of which she occasionally rested her head. The nurse sat beside her and the wardress recently transferred from Pentonville to Cardiff, on an adjacent seat.'

In Mr Paling's opening speech he referred to the Pace's unhappy marriage at which Beatrice began to cry. He went on to tell the court that the accused was still a teenager when she married Harry Pace and had given birth to ten children, five of whom were still alive. There followed an account of the whole history of Harry Pace's illness and death and all the medical evidence was meticulously summarised. It was considered most likely that at least three doses of arsenic were taken or administered between Christmas Day and 10 January when he died. Damage to his heart and liver were consistent with poisoning by arsenic some four or five months previously. Furthermore, it was possible to extract up to 8.7 grains of arsenic from a packet of sheep dip. When mixed with water the powder became a yellow fluid and if this was allowed to stand it would become clear on top—this, he described as 'very deadly, dangerous and poisonous fluid, which had the appearance of water, had no smell and a slight salt taste. I think you will have no doubt that the arsenic that was administered to the deceased had its origin in the sheep dip.'

As to how this poison got into Pace's body, went on Mr Paling, it was either by accident, suicide or murder. It was the opinion of the medical experts that arsenic would not be accidentally absorbed through healthy skin whilst dipping sheep—also, that

Pace had developed symptoms of poisoning long after his last dipping session in July, 1927.

As to the theory of suicide; although several witnesses had testified that Harry Pace was often depressed and had talked of killing himself, it is more usual for suicides to take one large dose rather then suffer repeated small doses. Mr Paling then asked the Bench to consider whether 'it was possible that Pace, who was ill, unable to grip anything, was helpless and in a dying condition, could have got out of bed, crossed the room, opened the drawer, which was, according to Mrs Pace, very difficult to open, take the dipping powder out of the box, put it in a receptacle, pour water over it, allow it to settle, and after drinking the fluid, dispose of the receptacle. In addition, he must take the poisonous fluid from the top which would have been difficult to do without taking in some of the sulphur contained in the sheep dip. No sulphur deposits were found in the body.'

Mr Paling then came to the third possibility—murder. Mrs Pace, he told the court, had every opportunity to poison her husband. She was often alone with him, prepared all his meals and knew that there was poisonous sheep dip in the house. As for motive, in her statements to the police she had complained of his cruelty throughout their married life. She had also admitted that any infidelity in the marriage 'was not confined to him'.

Reference was made to a visit to Pace by his mother shortly before he died; he had refused to drink from a glass of water by his bed and when his mother took a sip she said it tasted salty. Police had found one packet of sheep dip in the house but Mrs Pace had bought two packets on 22 July, 1927. Both these packets were seen in the cottage in August—where, asked Mr Paling, was the other?

After this long opening speech, three members of the Pace family were called to give evidence, during which Beatrice again broke down. The nurse attending her asked for water and she 'lifted the glass to her lips with trembling hands'. Shortly after, when Mrs Pritchard stated that Pace was in 'agonising pain' when he passed away, Mrs Pace almost fainted and was handed some smelling salts. Afterwards 'she leaned back in the doorway of the

163

dock and remained more or less in a state of semi-collapse for some time.' But she had recovered sufficiently by the end of the day's proceedings to throw a kiss to one of her relatives as she left the dock.

Outside the Court Beatrice's little daughter, Doris, became a common sight, often pacing up and down carrying a large doll in her arms, hoping for a glimpse of her mother as she arrived or left. When Beatrice arrived from Cardiff the following Monday, Doris was again waiting amongst a crowd on the pavement, but in vain for the car took a different route.

During the course of Monday Beatrice had to listen while Mr Paling read from the statements she had given the police during her long interrogation. One ran as follows:

'My husband and I have had a very unhappy life and I have left him on several occasions. He started to be cruel to me about two months after marriage. He tied me to the bedstead with rope apparently for nothing, and left me all day while he went to work, untying me when he came home. He also dug a hole in the garden and buried my baby's clothes. I ran to a neighbour's and told her what had occurred. I went back home and found all the doors locked and I slept outside on some straw. He repeatedly threatened to murder me with a razor. One day, in a temper, he got a hatchet, forced my head on the table and struck at me but I managed to get my head out of the way. The dent is still in the table now.'

The statement also described how Mrs Pace had been 'thrashed' when she was pregnant, and related the occasion when her husband had knocked out her dog's brains when one of his sheep was killed on the railway line. 'On this occasion,' she said, 'I think he was quite mad, as he went and got bricks and threw them at the chimney and knocked it off.'

The statement also referred to the unhappiness caused by her husband's 'immoral association with women' although Mr Paling refrained from reading two paragraphs in this section. Further reference was made to the disastrous Christmas Day. 'He had threatened to take his own life many times and now he has done it.' A little later she said 'Although he has been cruel to me at times I was very devoted to him and loved him until the end. He has repeatedly threatened to commit suicide. For years I have thought he was not in his right senses. He was cruel to his children. I have known him repeatedly kick them and bite their ears. Another strange thing he did was to clap his hands to his side and crow like a cockerel and at other times he would bark like a dog. He would sometimes sing most of the night. His imitation of the cockerel was so good that our cockerel would come on the wall and answer him.' The statement concluded: 'There are rumours that I have wrongly associated with other men but there is no truth in these rumours. It is my view that my husband poisoned himself. I emphatically say I know nothing about it.'

Dr Earengey, in Beatrice's defence, said that 'suspicion and antipathy on the part of the immediate relatives of the dead man, suspicion communicated to the police, enquiries made, and then rumours,' were responsible for the murder charge being brought against his client and he submitted to the magistrates that she not be brought to trial. Mrs Pace, he said, had been a 'devoted wife and nurse, leaving nothing undone.' The prosecution had built up their case on the supposition that Pace could not move from his bed 48 hours before death but Dr Dupré had argued he would have been able to get out of bed up to 12 hours before death, making it quite possible for him to reach the chest of drawers containing the dip.

Finally, Dr Earengey asked the magistrates to consider whether, if Beatrice Pace had poisoned her husband she would have left the bottle containing the sheep dip solution lying around in the bedroom. 'I cannot conceive the veriest baby taking such a line of conduct,' he scornfully concluded.

The magistrates, however, after deliberating for some fifty-eight minutes, decided that he was wrong and Beatrice Pace should stand trial for murder. Hearing this, Beatrice collapsed onto the floor of the dock.

'She was lifted by wardresses to the chair where she sat with her head between her knees and with her hands hanging limp and almost touching the floor. The Clerk read over the charge but she was insensible and could not have heard one word. There was a pause to see if she would recover but Dr Earengey had no objection to the proceedings going on.' Asked if the prisoner had anything to say in answer to the charge Dr Earengey said: 'On behalf of my client I plead not guilty and I reserve my defence.'

Beatrice Pace was taken back to Cardiff Prison in a closed car, crowds thronging the streets to catch a glimpse of her. Having already suffered the exceptionally long enquiry she had to cope with yet further separation from her children and once more listen to all the accusations, insinuations and character assassination at her trial at Gloucester Assizes in July. It is customary for the Attorney General to represent the Crown in major poison cases but in this instance it was the Solicitor-General, Sir Frank Boyd Merriman, who led the prosecution. Supporters of Beatrice Pace had subscribed to a fund for her defence and she was extremely fortunate to be able to enlist the services of one of the most distinguished young advocates of the day, Norman Birkett, who was willing to accept the brief for 'a reasonable fee of 100 guineas'.*

In his opening speech to the jury, the Solicitor-General pointed out that if Harry Pace had taken sheep dip in its original powder form there would have been a great deal of sulphur, as well as arsenic, in his body—large quantities of arsenic were found but no sulphur. Yet, if Pace did kill himself in a fit of depression, could they really believe that he would first go through the fiddling process of extracting the sulphur?

'If you are satisfied,' he said, 'that arsenic was administered in such a form that there was no sulphur in it, and if you are satisfied that that the man was not in a position, at any rate during the forty-eight hours before his death, to get rid of the sulphur himself, that is the end of the theory of suicide.'

When called as a witness, Sir William Willcox remained adamant that Pace could not have been poisoned by contact with the sheep dip, no matter how careless he might have been. Pace's mother, however, by Birkett's careful questioning, gave credence

---

* Norman Birkett, KC, featured in a number of famous murder cases in the 1930's. A wealthy Roumanian gentleman, Mr Jonescu, donated £500 to the fund for Beatrice Pace's defence.

to the suicide theory by admitting that one of her other sons had committed suicide.

Elton Pace, unsurprisingly, was not so helpful to the defence and when asked about Beatrice's reaction to her husband's death, he banged his fists on the witness stand: 'She was as unconcerned as this here box,' he retorted.

The case for the Crown was closed shortly before lunch on the fifth day of the trial. Immediately after the court was reconvened, Norman Birkett submitted that his client had no case to answer.

'The scientific evidence,' he said, 'is consistent with administration of the poison by the deceased equally with any other theory.' As for the prosecution's suggestion that, as Mrs Pace had been the one to prepare all her husband's food, she must be the prime suspect—this was a preposterous assumption, under which 'every wife in the country' could be suspected of poisoning their husbands. Surprisingly, perhaps, after the view of the Coroner's and Magistrates Courts, Mr Justice Horridge agreed and delivered the following ruling:

'No case has been more thoroughly investigated and no case could have been conducted with more scrupulous fairness by the prosecution than this. I think the Solicitor-General did quite right in leaving this matter to me, and I am of the opinion that it would not be safe to ask the jury to proceed further with it.'

The judge then directed the jury to return a verdict of 'Not Guilty'. As the verdict was delivered Beatrice sat with her head bowed, weeping. She looked dazed as her solicitor leaned across and took her hand but after a moment or two she walked across to Norman Birkett and thanked him warmly. It was at this point that members of the public burst into a chorus of cheers, waving their handkerchiefs and throwing their hats into the air.

Outside the court-house a huge crowd had gathered and as a sour-faced Elton Pace pushed his way through the crowd people jeered and shook their fists at him; undaunted and obviously still convinced of his sister-in-law's guilt he looked at them with contempt.

Beatrice Pace followed shortly after, free at last to join her young family and free, above all, from an erratic bully of a man who had abused her throughout their marriage, made her life a misery and probably ended his own.

In a biography of Norman Birkett, H. Montgomery Hyde says this:

'It may well be that Harry Pace accidentally killed himself. Nor can there be any doubt that in the circumstances the trial jury returned the right verdict in this case, although some observers may possibly have been tempted to adopt the opinion expressed by a distinguished surgeon* with regard to a similar case of poisoning forty years previously that "once it was all over, she should have told us, in the interests of science, how she did it."'

---

* Sir James Paget, Sergeant-Surgeon to Queen Victoria and Consulting Surgeon at St Bartholomew's Hospital. He was referring to the acquittal of Adelaide Bartlett at the Old Bailey in 1886. She had been charged with the murder of her husband with liquid chloroform and was brilliantly defended by Edward Clarke, QC. The case is the subject of the author's book *The Pimlico Murder: The Strange Case of Adelaide Bartlett*.

XII

Who killed Simon Dale?

One of the most fascinating unsolved cases of the twentieth century must surely be the murder of Simon Dale, the story behind which was so extraordinary that it attracted nationwide interest. It is a compelling tale with all the ingredients of the most imaginative fiction—of love turned to hate, a mansion house and a humble cottage, great wealth and frugal living, deception and intrigue—and at the very centre, an enigmatic woman, the Baroness Cecilia Susan de Stempel, who, with her cool and haughty manner, was soon dubbed by the Press 'the Ice Queen'. It was, said Mr Anthony Palmer, the prosecuting counsel at the subsequent murder trial, a story of 'high society and low deeds'. Little wonder it became headline news for nearly every newspaper in the country during the unusually hot summer of 1989. Yet the complete story only came to light after Dale's murder in the autumn of 1987.

Heath House, near Hopton Heath, Leintwardine, is a Jacobean mansion that stands deep in the brooding Shropshire countryside, facing the magnificent hills and mountains of Wales. The house itself, built in the first half of the seventeenth century, with its simple but pleasantly proportioned rose-brick facade, has an air of mystery about it, a timeless, waiting presence and the shuttered windows lend the house a certain watchfulness.*

---

* In 1968, a local doctor, Alan Beach, was shot whilst sitting in his car at the gateway to Heath House by Arthur Prime, who blamed the doctor for his wife's death. Prime was found to be insane at the time of the shooting and served his life sentence in a psychiatric unit.

Simon Dale, a sixty eight year old architect, was almost blind, yet he managed to live alone, restricting himself to a bedroom on the first floor, the kitchen and one or two rooms on the ground floor. The rest of the vast house, with more than thirty rooms, was empty and desolate, with most of the fine furniture gone. Fitting rather uneasily into the centre of the house is a heavy oak staircase, said to have been transplanted from Hopton Castle in 1644, after it was was rendered uninhabitable by Royalists during the Civil War.

Dale was a large, gregarious man, with a domed head, which was bald save for tufts of white hair above his ears. His voice was sonorous and booming and, once his interest was engaged, his conversation could be lively and amusing. He was an intellectual but unorthodox man, fond of debate and forceful in his views, some might say opinionated, and enjoyed the company of a small group of loyal friends who called for tea and generally kept an eye on him. Far from being housebound, however, he often made the journey along the twisting country lanes to Hopton Railway Station, where he would catch the train to Shrewsbury to use the public library.

He also managed to obtain lifts to Leominster where he would pester the District Planning Office or argue a point with some other authority he saw fit to challenge. He was fanatically interested in archaeology, medicine and history, Arthurian history in particular, and had many contacts with similar interests. He was convinced that there was a strong link between King Arthur and the area and that Heath House was possibly the site of the ancient capital of the ancient kingdom of Powys. At the time of his death he was hoping to generate enough interest to instigate major excavations of the site.*

He was also passionately interested in optics and brain function and had recently contacted the Radar Establishment at Malvern to discuss some of his theories. Despite his disability, he coped remarkably well; he employed a housekeeper for two hours a

---

* Shortly before his death Dale had two articles on this theme published in the *British Archaeological Monthly*.

Simon Dale in the doorway of Heath House

week but managed to cook for himself, even making his own jam and marmalade. His vision was reduced to a pin-prick but with the aid of contact lenses, thick spectacles and a powerful magnifying glass he was able to read a little but for his writing and copious correspondence he relied on the assistance of his band of helpers—and, it must be said, welcomed their visits to alleviate what must have been, despite his friends, a fairly solitary existence.

One such helper was Giselle Wall, an ex-teacher from the village of Kempton, some six miles away. She had worked for Dale since May 1986 and was typing out one of his historical articles. On Sunday, 13 September, 1987, having promised to deliver the work she had completed, she rang Dale several times but received no answer. She decided, however, to go as planned and arrived at Heath House at 4.20 p.m. Parking her car at the back of the house she went round to the kitchen entrance. The geranium red door was shut but not locked. She noticed that the shutters were still closed which was unusual. But when she opened the door and saw the light was still on she knew that something was wrong. Once inside the narrow passage she could feel a fierce heat coming from the kitchen accompanied by an acrid smell of burning. Stepping over a broken deck-chair (in the folds of which lay a heavy bunch of keys) lying across the lobby, she looked inside the kitchen—there, sprawled on the floor, half jammed against the door was the body of Simon Dale. He was lying on his back and blood had congealed in a pool on the floor around his head. There were marks on his forehead and his arms were bent backwards with his hands on his chest, his fingers clutching his jumper.

Horrified, Giselle Wall ran from the house and drove to Heath Lodge, a quarter of a mile away, the home of Mike Hollis, an antique dealer. Thinking that Simon Dale had suffered a stroke or a heart attack he rang for an ambulance, which arrived at Heath House within fifteen minutes. Seeing the red hot ring on the cooker the ambulance men turned it off but found the switch was faulty. After a cursory glance around the stifling kitchen they guessed it was a case of murder. They knew from experience that the position of the arms and hands was one associated with a broken neck and there were signs of a violent struggle. In addition to the blood on the floor near the body more could be seen sprayed across the walls in the passageway and the kitchen, and on the large refectory table in the centre of the room.

The police were contacted immediately. The ambulance men were to say later that the heat in the room was appalling and as decomposition of the body had already begun, the smell was sickening. Detective Constable Geoffrey Daniels, from Leominster CID, arrived within minutes whilst a doctor, Margaret Davies, confirmed that Simon Dale was dead. A team of police photographers set to work recording the scene in every detail and a video was also made. It became clear that Simon Dale had been disturbed whilst preparing his evening meal; in the overheated oven they found the charred remains of a toad-in-the-hole. On the table were the runner beans and courgettes he had yet to prepare and on a work surface near the sink were five sherry glasses; three showed the remains of sherry, one was cracked and one, of a different design, was half full.

After the arrival of Detective Inspector Derek Matthews, the drive was cordoned off. Detective Superintendent David Cole was assigned to take charge of the case, which was to involve dozens of officers, including, at a later stage, the Fraud Squad. Further investigation at Heath House suggested that robbery was not the motive for the murder. There were no signs of a forced entry and Dale's wallet containing £25 was still in the back pocket of his trousers and he was still wearing his gold cuff links.

Over the next few hours the police interviewed Giselle Wall, Mike Hollis and the Spencer family, who lived in a cottage behind Heath House. From Jenny Spencer they learned that Simon Dale's ex-wife, Susan, was living in a cottage at Docklow and that there was a long-running dispute over possession of Heath House. It was nearly midnight by the time the body of Simon Dale was taken to Hereford County Hospital for examination by pathologist Dr Peter Acland and it was only then, nearly eight hours after the murder was discovered, that the police decided to contact his ex-wife. Fifty-three year old Susan had become a Baroness after her divorce from Dale and subsequent re-marriage, twelve years later, to Baron Michael de Stempel and had retained the title after that marriage was also dissolved, in 1986.

Since 1977, the Baroness had been living some twenty-six miles away in Docklow, a small community consisting of a few houses, a church and a pub scattered alongside the A44 between Leominster and Worcester. She and three of her five children from her marriage to Dale—Marcus, aged 26, Sophia, 25 and 23 year old Simon, were living in one of a pair of semi-detached estate workers' dwellings called Forresters Cottages. With characteristic style, the Baroness renamed her cottage Forresters Hall.

At 12.30, in the early hours of Monday, 14 September, the police knocked on the door of the Docklow cottage. At first no one answered but the door was eventually opened by Marcus, looking anxious and dishevelled, wearing a jumper over his pyjamas. Looking through the doorway the police were surprised to see that, belying its humble and worn exterior the cottage was crammed with expensive antiques—fine furniture, paintings, chandelier and a plethora of expensive Oriental carpets. The Baroness came downstairs, fully dressed in a suit, and invited the police to come in. Her daughter, Sophia, was also present, wearing her nightclothes—so, too, was her youngest son, Simon, dressed in jeans and a jumper.

The Baroness was not, in fact, the least bit surprised to see the police officers for she had just made Marcus telephone the Leominster police station to complain that someone was banging on her door. They were making such a noise and commotion, she said, she thought it was a party of drunks. With the element of farce that pervades the whole case she was told that her visitors *were* the police and advised to open the door. She later complained about having to endure the 'inane' conversations of the police that night who, she added, looked 'incredibly furtive and had such an impertinent manner about them'.

When told by Detective Inspector Matthews that 'there was a problem at Heath House' the Baroness showed no surprise. She asked if Dale had burned the place down, inferring that it was the sort of thing he might well do to spite her and prevent it being sold. When told that her ex-husband was dead she showed no emotion but merely asked if the house had been broken into. Later, when recalling the scene that night for the jury at Worcester Crown Court, Matthews said that the Baroness was 'calm and collected', Marcus was 'nervous and belligerent' and Sophia was 'bubbly and talkative'. The youngest son, Simon, was 'quiet and disinterested'. The Baroness was to explain later that she was able to maintain her self-control because as a child she had been strictly trained not to show emotion.

Before leaving Forresters Hall, Matthews took possession of a highly polished brass poker he found in the Baroness's grey Peugeot estate, which was parked in the driveway. Whilst inside the cottage he had also noticed a letter addressed to Lady Illingworth lying on the floor. On asking who she was Marcus replied, 'Aunt Puss'. The discovery of the connection between the Baroness and her aunt, Margaret, Lady Illingworth,* was to have dramatic repercussions and eventually lead to a complicated enquiry, a charge of forgery, theft and conspiracy to defraud, and a protracted and very expensive trial.

Back at Heath House, a forensic team led by Dr Norman Weston, from the Home Office forensic science laboratory in Birmingham, began the painstaking and time-consuming task of searching Heath House, the adjoining cottage which was used to store gardening equipment and the five acre garden. Dozens of hair, blood and fibre samples were taken from the kitchen, and every other room in the house was searched with infinite care. A number of experiments were also carried out—including one in which a pig was roasted to simulate a human body undergoing the same degree of intense and sustained heat that had been present in the kitchen after Dale's murder—others involved the monitoring of deliberately burned toad-in-the-hole. The time of death was eventually established as between 8.30 p.m. and 9.00 p.m. on Friday, 11 September, and the pathologist concluded that,

* Margaret, Lady Illingworth, widow of Lord Illingworth of Denton, a Bradford wool merchant, ex-Cabinet minister and Postmaster General.

Heath House

although Simon Dale had suffered five blows to the head, he was killed by a vicious blow that had crushed the larynx, causing him to inhale his own blood and die from respiratory failure.

The enquiry also resulted in a detailed account of Friday, 11 September, the day Simon Dale died. Despite the murky weather, his ex-wife, Marcus and Sophia had been busy working on the outside of the house. Sophia had been on the mobile scaffold painting window frames whilst Susan and Marcus worked in the garden, which had become completely overgrown. This had been their routine for months—since the spring of 1986; frustrated at not being able to work on the interior of her house, the Baroness was concentrating on the outside. Occasionally, she and Simon would exchange a few choice insults through open windows, but as a general rule they avoided each other, too embittered even to argue. Over the last few years the dispute had become a battle for dominance—the Baroness, significantly, chose to wear a military style camouflage jacket and had armed herself with a jemmy or case-opener when working in the garden. She said she had bought it to tackle the brambles that had invaded the driveway and to clear away the broken glass. She added later that she had taken to carrying it as protection, partly as a joke, but also because she was afraid her ex-husband might attack her.

After going to Leominster in the morning and working all afternoon with one of his assistants, Simon Dale had four known visitors that evening—Ben Scott, who shared his enthusiasm for archaeology, accompanied by Susan Evans, who used to be one of his helpers, with her two young sons. Scott testified later that they were unable to drive round to the front of the house in their caravanette because someone had placed a water butt under the archway, blocking their way. Suddenly, he said, the angry face of the Baroness appeared at the window of the car, declaring that she was the 'mad former wife', that Simon was himself mad, that the upstairs of the house was full of fleas, the downstairs was filthy and Dale was 'slumming it' in the kitchen. Finally she said: 'What's the point in seeing him? He'll be out in a month.'

Taken aback by this unprovoked tirade, Ben Scott and Susan Evans put the alarm on the caravanette and, walking round the back of the house to the kitchen, joined Simon Dale for a tour of the house and a glass of sherry. In the meantime, the two lads, larking about on a pair of rocking horses, managed to dislodge one of the tails. They were then dispatched to play in the garden whilst Simon and his guests talked about archaeology in general and his Arthurian theories in particular. Simon appeared to be in good spirits, excited about his latest projects and unperturbed by the fact that his ex-wife was still in the grounds. When told about the incident with Susan as they arrived he merely shrugged and said 'she always talked like that', as if he was accustomed, almost amused, by it all.

It was about a quarter past eight and already dark by the time Ben Scott, Susan Evans and the boys had left. Sophia, tired and wet from working in the drizzle all day, had already gone back to Docklow and Marcus, just before leaving, had gone to feed his bees. By this time a breeze was picking up so he decided to place bricks on the hives to secure the roofs. He was gone for ten minutes. When he returned he and his mother drove back to Docklow, arriving soon after nine o'clock. By this time, Simon Dale was already dead.

The Baroness later admitted that she and her children generally left Heath House about six in the evening, but on that Friday she had stayed later as she was anxious to see the visitors leave the premises before returning to Docklow. She was naturally concerned about the boys running loose and possibly causing more damage and, moreover, she felt that Simon had no right to show people around her house and discuss the possibility of archaeological excavations on the site without her consent.

The Baroness told the police she spent the rest of Friday evening in her bedroom watching an adaptation of the Agatha Christie novel *Murder at the Vicarage*. The next morning, Marcus and Sophia had left very early to visit friends in Kent and the Baroness, as she did most weekends, and young Simon went over to Heath House. But she made two journeys. She wished to saw up some logs and couldn't fit the saw bench and all the equipment in one load. On arriving for the second time she broke her usual habit and parked her car at the front of the house, instead of round the back near the archway and cottage; she noticed nothing unusual on either visit. The shutters were closed, but she made no point of checking as she claimed she was frightened of Simon Dale. She did, however, go to check Marcus's hives to ensure the roofs were weighted down with bricks, as the weather had turned quite blustery.

Despite a massive enquiry, involving more than a hundred police officers, two months went by without the finding of any clues to the identity of Dale's killer. Unfortunately, the family living close to the house said they had heard and seen nothing unusual on the evening of the murder. After appealing for information from the public the police tried to trace a red car seen near Heath House at ten thirty on the night of the murder. About the same time several witnesses had also seen a young hitch-hiker, with long hair, a red head-band and a rucksack thumbing a lift as he walked along the road near Heath House. Others seeing an elderly, grey-haired man walking near Heath House on the Saturday morning after the murder; a middle-aged woman, having left a young girl in the passenger seat of her car, was also seen looking across at the house from the side of the road; but despite appeals to the public and even a reconstruction of Dale's murder on BBC Television's Crimewatch, the young hitchhiker was never found and no other leads were produced.

Unknown to the public, in addition to the murder enquiry, members of the West Mercia Fraud Squad, led by Detective Inspector Mike Cowley, were busy investigating the finances of the Baroness. When they questioned her closely about her aunt, Lady Illingworth, (known within the family as Aunt Puss, on account of her fondness for cats), they found that she had once been an exceedingly rich woman, accustomed to every luxury, and famous for the grand parties she gave at her house in Grosvenor Square in the 30's and 40's. But, they were told, after staying at the cottage in Docklow, she had been reduced to living on state benefits in an old peoples' home in Hereford. She had died of Alzheimer's disease in 1986 and was cremated, (despite her wish to be buried in Bradford beside her husband), having left a will bequeathing much of her fortune to Susan de Stempel. They learned, too, of the involvement of the Baroness's second husband, Baron Michael de Stempel.

On Monday, 7 December, 1987, as a result of these enquiries, the Baroness, Marcus and Sophia were arrested on suspicion of fraud and taken to Hereford Central Police Station for questioning. Their names were not revealed to the public until a week later when they, together with Baron Michael de Stempel, appeared at Hereford City Magistrates Court charged with conspiring to defraud Lady Illingworth. Their application for bail was refused.

Meanwhile the murder investigation was still under way and the police were learning a great deal more about Susan de Stempel's family, her early life and first marriage. She was born Susan Cecilia Mary Wilberforce, in May, 1934, the great great grand-daughter of William Wilberforce. Her mother, Cecilia, née Dormer, was a member of a prominent Catholic family from Buckinghamshire, one, according to Burke's Peerage & Baronetcy, of the 'greatest antiquity'. Her father, William Wilberforce, Lady Illingworth's younger brother, was killed in action during the Second World War. The year was 1943 and

Susan, at nine years old, had already been a boarder at St Mary's Convent at Ascot since the age of five. Her brother, William John, but called John, was four years older than Susan and was destined to inherit Markington Hall, the seventeenth century family home in Yorkshire. After leaving Oxford he joined the Foreign Office, later to become British High Commissioner for Cyprus.

After an unremarkable school career in which her main talent was for music, Susan Wilberforce became one of the debutantes of the early fifties. As her mother had remarried and gone to live in Scotland it was her aunt, Lady Illingworth, who organised her 'coming out' from her lavish house in Grosvenor Square and generally treated her niece with great generosity.

When Susan reached the age of eighteen, she and her brother had amicably agreed to divide their inheritance—John retained Markington Hall whilst Susan received some 2,000 acres of land, which included farms and a quarry. Even the furniture was divided between the two.

At the age of twenty-three, Susan was invited to a friend's house for dinner and met Simon Dale. At thirty-eight, he was a sophisticated character with a passion for his chosen profession—architecture. Though not handsome in a conventional way, he was charming and courteous and, at six foot three he cut an imposing figure. Unfortunately, his sight was already poor and he had no money. But Susan, perhaps bored with conventional society, fell in love with him and, despite strong family disapproval, married him at St James's Church, Clerkenwell, in August 1957. They lived in South Kensington for a while, where, a year later their first son, Alexander, was born. It was soon after this that they discovered a semi-derelict mansion deep in the Shropshire countryside—Heath House, which Susan bought for £2,000 in 1959, three days before it was due to be demolished.

Little were they to know that it would become the cause of so much bitterness between them and result in a lengthy and acrimonious battle for possession. But at the time they were blissfully happy, determined to use Susan's money and Simon's skill to restore the house and raise their family in an idyllic rural setting.

Parts of the house were uninhabitable and for the first five years they lived on the top floor. Work on the house became a constant drain on Susan's inheritance; she gradually sold off her furniture from Markington, piece by piece, but before long the money began to run out. Simon had never earned very much as an architect and, as his eyesight deteriorated, he rarely received commissions and the situation became desperate. But for the first few years they were happy, with the energy and optimism of pioneers; a second son, Sebastian, was born in 1960 and a year later, Marcus—then in 1962, Sophia, and finally, in 1964, the last of their children, Simon.

Sadly, as time passed, everything changed. Understandably, perhaps, as Dale's eyesight worsened, frustration made him morose and difficult. As for Susan, the strain of bringing up five young children in isolation, with few labour saving amenities and very little money, had begun to take its toll. Before long they began to loathe each other and all the warmth and laughter of the early years had gone, to be replaced by an all consuming bitterness. In 1972, Susan began divorce proceedings and was awarded a decree nisi a year later on the grounds of 'unreasonable behaviour'. Part of the divorce agreement was that Heath House should be sold and the proceeds divided. Of immense importance to this case was the added stipulation that Simon Dale could remain in the house until a buyer was found and contracts between vendor and purchaser had been exchanged. It was a clause that was to spawn the most bitter, and sometimes vicious battle between the two, one that only ended in Simon's death and Susan's arrest fifteen years later.

Susan remained in the house a further two months but then, in September 1973, unable to stand it any longer, she left. 'One day,' she said later, 'I just picked up my handbag, got in the car and went.'

She drove directly to Mellington House, her mother's house in Weobley. By this time the children were at boarding schools, partly financed by Lady Illingworth's brother, Robert, known as 'Uncle Wee' on account of his large size. When Cecilia died a year later, Susan and the children remained in the house until, in accordance with her mother's will, it had to be sold, her brother John being the major beneficiary. Susan inherited a residual legacy of £20,000 which brought her about £1,000 a year and the furniture was divided equally with her brother. Once again, her brother got the house and she was homeless; she and the children stayed for a while at Markington Hall but, failing to settle in Yorkshire, they went instead to Ross-on-Wye where she lived in a small flat rented from friends. By this time Susan had relinquished the name of Dale in favour of Wilberforce and the children followed suit on reaching the age of eighteen.

By the autumn of 1977, Susan and her three youngest children had moved to the three-bedroomed cottage at Docklow. Heath House had been on the market for three years and, although there had been a number of prospective buyers, Simon Dale seemed to have gone out of his way to obstruct the sale and, despite a volley of solicitors' letters, the house remained unsold.

It was at this point that Susan's long-standing friendship with Baron Michael Victor Jossif Walter de Stempel developed further. She had met him through her brother, when he and the Baron were at Oxford in 1952; he became an amusing member of her circle during her debutante season in London and they had a brief affair during which she maintained he asked her to marry him many times.

They had remained friends over the years but by now the Baron had two children from his first marriage and was currently living with his second wife, Francesca Tesi, by whom he had a son. Michael's father had been a Russian aristocrat, one of many titled émigrés forced to flee their country during the Revolution; his mother was from a family of diamond merchants, and Michael was their only child. After his parents' divorce, 'Mishka', at the age of five, the epitome of the poor little rich boy, became the subject of a harrowing and much publicised custody case in 1937.

Impressions of Michael de Stempel are mixed; to some he might appear a rather ludicrous figure with a strutting self-importance and a voice once described as sounding rather like a 'broken Stradivarius', or, as Kate Wharton suggests in her book

Blood Money: The Story of the Baroness de Stempel, like 'the high bleat of a lost sheep'. Past acquaintances have described him as boastful, bigoted and obsessed with money and titles—John Wilberforce, in a police statement, described him as 'an eccentric with an obsessive interest in titles and the Almanach de Gotha'. Even his own defence counsel at his subsequent trial branded him 'a congenital liar', 'a monumental snob' and 'a man without courage'. On the other hand he is considered by many, mainly women who feel the need to mother him, to be a vulnerable, harmlessly eccentric and amusing man of great charm and generosity.

In the meantime Sophia had gone to work in London; she stayed with Lady Illingworth, who had moved from Grosvenor Square to a large flat in York House, Kensington, which she shared with an elderly cousin and a housekeeper. While Sophia was there she persuaded Aunt Puss who, at the age of 82, was becoming progressively senile, to go to Docklow for a holiday. Her chauffeur for more than twenty years described her as a 'lovely old lady' who looked 'just like the Queen Mother'. On 29 February, 1984, she arrived at Forresters Hall a very rich woman and left on 6 December 1984 a relatively poor one. In June of that year she had apparently made a will leaving the bulk of her estate to Susan. Much of her wealth in the form of jewellry, antique furniture, silver, paintings and other artifacts were subsequently found at the cottage in Docklow when the police called with the news that Simon Dale had been murdered.

Before the arrival of Aunt Puss, Michael de Stempel, now divorced from his second wife and expecting a legacy, had already become a frequent visitor to Docklow and regularly helped to pay the bills. By this time, Sophia had come back to look after Aunt Puss and the cottage had become grossly over-crowded. At one point things were so bad the Baron slept in a tent on the lawn though it was suggested by his former wife that he and Susan spent an inordinate amount of time in bed discussing their pedigrees.

After various setbacks and procrastinations Susan eventually married Michael de Stempel in St Helier, Jersey, on 11 September 1984, and became Baroness de Stempel. She now had the man she wanted, a title and the 'family inheritance' from Aunt Puss. She was also in the frustrating position of having a fine house which she was unable to either occupy or sell. Encouraged by the Baron she made a more concerted effort to get Simon out. Her letters to her solicitor—which he found extraordinary and amusing—increased but without immediate result. Equally frustrating, the marriage to the Baron did not last long. When he returned to London—by which time Lady Illingworth had died—he initiated divorce proceedings and on a subsequent visit to Docklow various events bordering on the surreal resulted in the Baroness trying to have Michael certified.

Such was the complicated state of affairs prior to Simon Dale's death on 11 September 1987. Public response had been disappointing and by December the murder enquiry was still in progress. Every inch of Heath House and the surrounding countryside had been searched and countless interviews given. Then, on 7 January 1988, there was a dramatic development. *The Daily Mail* printed the following announcement:

'A baroness and two of her children were accused yesterday of murdering her former husband who was found battered to death in his country mansion. Baroness Susan Cecilia de Stempel, fifty-three, her son Xenophon Marcus Wilberforce, twenty-six and daughter Georgina Sophia Wilberforce, twenty-five, who live at Forresters Hall, Docklow, Herefordshire, were all remanded in custody for a week by Hereford Magistrates... The Baroness appeared in court in a checked shirt and anorak, and was described as a housewife. Her son was described as self-employed and her daughter as unemployed... All three were also accused, along with Baron Michael de Stempel of Upper Park Road, London, of plotting to defraud the Baroness's late aunt, Lady Margaret Illingworth...'

Both Marcus and Sophia seemed remarkably young for their years, appearing more like adolescents than adults. The Baroness appeared diffident and withdrawn as those thoroughly bored with the whole affair.

But on 27 January 1988, at Hereford Magistrates Court, after many hours of interrogation, the charges of murder against

The Baroness

Marcus and Sophia were withdrawn. The charge against the Baroness remained. When arrested and charged with murder she had said: 'I have nothing to say whatsoever.' And even, after nine hours of taped police interviews she remained in complete control and coolly denied that she was in any way responsible for her ex-husband's death. All three were further remanded on the charge of fraud. So, too, was the Baron, incarcerated in Gloucester prison, although less than a month later he was granted bail of £240,000 by a High Court judge in London. Marcus and Sophia were not allowed the same privilege until 15 April, each in the sum of £190,000. The Baroness, however, was to remain in custody for a very long time. Such were the complications of the concurrent murder and fraud cases that committal proceedings were not scheduled until the beginning of the following year—to be held at Bromyard Magistrates Court.

On the day of the hearing, Wednesday, 4 January 1989, the weather was bitterly cold—far too cold for the antiquated plumbing of the Courthouse lavatories—they froze, as did the journalists and photographers waiting since early morning for the Baroness to arrive. Local and national newspapers had already guessed that the case would continue and lead, they hoped, to a sensational story. The object of the committal hearing was to establish whether there was a prima facie case to answer. Whether or not the case should go to trial rested with the magistrates after hearing all the evidence for and against the accused. David Crigman, QC, presented the case for the prosecution whilst Anthony Hughes appeared for the defence. In the course of his summary of the case, Crigman said this:

'The place of the killing was the kitchen of Heath House. That is the house over which the defendant and her ex-husband had fought for over fourteen years, in which the victim lived, and the defendant was despairing of ever getting her hands on the property again. The prosecution says that the evidence discloses an obvious case for this defendant to answer. One, she had a deep-seated hatred of the deceased. Two, she had expressed a wish to see him killed [this had been mentioned casually]. Three, there is evidence of irrational behaviour over a long period of time. Four, there is a link between her and one of the likely murder weapons.* Five, on the night when Mr Dale was last seen alive, the defendant was surreptitiously hiding in the grounds of Heath House, waiting for visitors of the deceased to leave. Six, she had a very well-used means of access to the house and this is a case of violence where there is no forcible entry to the house ...'

From the statements of Ben Scott and Susan Evans the court was given a detailed account of the night Simon Dale died. The prosecution also questioned Michael de Stempel at some length about a telephone call he received early one morning from either the Baroness or Sophia, (he really couldn't be sure as they sounded so alike), informing him that Simon Dale was dead. He was also unable to remember whether the call was made on Saturday, 12 September, 1984, the day after Dale died and before

---

* This refers to the jemmy or case-opener which the Baroness used in the garden. Forensic examination revealed no trace of blood, hair or body tissue whatsoever and also indicated that the jemmy had *not* been recently cleaned.

his body was discovered, or the following Saturday, 19 September.

Statements from other witnesses were also read during the hearing—which was restricted to two days instead of three because of the unusually cold weather and the unfortunate loss of the lavatories. As the proceedings drew to a close Anthony Hughes dismissed the case as a 'colourful, picturesque tale that would fit happily into a novel or soap opera.... There is no direct evidence to link this lady with the case.' He reminded the court that although the forensic team had searched her clothing, her car and the cottage at Docklow they had come up with nothing whatever to link her with the murder of Simon Dale.

He did not dispute the fact that the Baroness was waiting in the gardens of Heath House that night but not, he suggested, with malicious intent but because she was protecting her property—anxious about Simon's schemes for digging beneath the foundations or turning it into a conference centre for mediaeval historians. It was, after all, he went on, her house, not his, and surely her concern was perfectly reasonable?

Finally, he asked the court to consider the sherry glasses found at the scene of the murder. There were five glasses in all—Ben Scott, Susan Evans and Simon Dale had drunk from three, one was cracked and presumably discarded—so who had drunk from the fifth glass? Had there been another visitor in the kitchen of Heath House that evening after the others had left?

The magistrates took seventy-five minutes to come to the decision that there *was* a case for the defendant to answer. As they gave their verdict the Baroness stood, straight backed, her face a mask. The trial was set for Tuesday, 18 July, 1989, at Worcester Crown Court and as the reporters raced to the nearby telephones the Baroness was led away to Pucklehurst Remand Centre to contemplate her fate.

The trial of the Baroness de Stempel was pure theatre. The vast entrance hall of the Court at Worcester—with its monstrous statue of Queen Victoria standing full square on the forecourt—was humming with small groups of robed barristers engaged in earnest conversation, (rewarding their audience with the occasional disdainful look and dramatic sweep of their gowns). Between the groups scurried grey-suited gentlemen with tense faces and strapped books under their arms. The atmosphere was one of nervous anticipation common to murder trials. In one corner, looking ridiculously out of place, was a trestle table from which some anonymous ladies were serving cups of tea.

Outside, a long black limousine drew to a halt alongside the grand entrance. The drama was about to begin. In the hall the talking subsided and everyone stood still—a hush, broken by the trumpeters heralding the arrival of the High Court Judge, Mr Justice Owen.*

Lesser mortals were assigned to the converging and treacherously narrow stairs that led up to the public gallery, which was equipped with five rows of extremely uncomfortable wooden benches. Directly opposite, on a dais deep in the well of the court, was the High Judge's chair; above it was a very tall canopy, topped by a painted plaster crown, on which rested a substantial layer of dust. Behind this was a wall of multi-paned windows through which flocks of pigeons kept up a chorus of coos throughout the proceedings, intermittently drowned by a sudden rise in the level of noise from the traffic outside and on one occasion by a deafening cacophony from an off-course aircraft.

Along the right hand gallery were crammed members of the local and national press, pens poised; below them sat the jurors and in the centre of the court was the dock with steps leading down into the cells below. It was here that the Baroness de Stempel sat throughout the eleven days of her trial, which began on Tuesday, 18 July, 1989; she invariably wore a high-necked style of blouse, a floral skirt and a cotton jacket, either striped or plain, but blue in colour. As the weather was blisteringly hot during the whole of the trial she usually removed her jacket and occasionally, in the stifling heat of the afternoon sessions, would also remove her shoes and sit in her stockinged feet.

---

* Sir John Owen. In 1990, he presided over the first case under English law in which a man was found quilty of raping his wife.

Throughout the trial she was accompanied by one or two wardresses, who, with their robust build, cropped hair and crisp uniform, made the Baroness appear very pale and thin, almost ethereal by comparison. The lack of empathy between these women and their prisoner was quite evident and for the most part they stared stonily ahead and barely glanced in her direction.

During most of the proceedings the Baroness appeared impassive, disinterested even. Occasionally she would raise her spectacles to her eyes and stare at a witness or member of the court as though inspecting an insect that had momentarily caught her attention. But as the jurors, eight men and four women, filed into the court each day, (armed with an ample supply of boiled sweets), they were rewarded with a more penetrating look. Now and then the Baroness took up the small notebook and the pen—which she kept in her spectacle case, placed neatly on the chair beside her—and wrote musical notes from the bottom of the page to the top. All her actions were slowly and meticulously performed and her self-control in such an appallingly stressful situation was remarkable.

The first part of the proceedings was taken up with legal matters concerning the forthcoming fraud charge, after which Anthony Palmer, QC, a very astute and experienced advocate acting on behalf of the Crown, rose to instruct the jury on the relevant facts of the case. The whole preamble was told in great detail, in his precise, well-modulated voice, emphasising every aspect of the case he felt reflected badly on the prisoner. The Baroness's defence counsel, Anthony Arlidge, QC,* bespectacled and deceptively benign, listened attentively whilst the judge made copious notes.

On the third day the jurors were obliged to adjourn to a room above the court and watch the edited police video made shortly after the murder was discovered. The public were, of course, excluded but the Baroness, it was later reported, watched the gruesome spectacle of her ex-husband's bloodied corpse on the

* Anthony Palmer prosecuted Eddie Browning in the Marie Wilks case in 1989; Anthony Arlidge prosecuted Jeremy Bamber at Chelmsford Crown Court, in 1986.

floor of the kitchen at Heath House impassively. When questioned the following day about her unnaturally calm response she said that, on the contrary, she had felt sick on seeing the video and was struggling, as she had been trained to do, to control her emotions and avoid being sick.

A number of witnesses were called: members of West Mercia Police, Dale's cleaning lady, one of his helpers and Adrian Tindall, an archaeologist who had visited Heath House at Simon Dale's request. He said that as he approached the house Susan had 'emerged from the undergrowth' with the case-opener over her arm, which, she told him, she carried for her own protection.

Ben Scott also took the stand; a tanned, debonair sort of fellow, sporting an impressive handle-bar moustache, as white as his hair. He was questioned at length about his meeting with Simon Dale at Heath House on the night he died. He said that from their conversation he gathered that Dale was expecting another visitor at some time, either that same evening or perhaps on another day entirely—he was unable to be more explicit than that. He stood to attention and clicked his heels, military fashion, as he bowed his head to the judge before leaving the court.

The chief witness on the Friday was the highly experienced forensic scientist, Dr Norman Weston. He hoisted a huge folder of notes onto the witness box and proceeded to tell the court that no less than sixty-four fibre and hair samples had been taken from the kitchen at Heath House—there were a number of red woollen strands and a sandy coloured hair that had not been accounted for, yet despite these exhaustive searches and microscopic examination of samples taken from the Baroness's clothing, her car, the jemmy at Heath House, the poker she had polished and even the chimney and drains of the cottage at Docklow, *he had found nothing whatsoever to link her forensicly with the crime.* As he left the court he winked triumphantly in the direction of the dock but received no discernable response from either the wardress or the Baroness.

Also called was Richard Sax, one of the Baroness's long-suffering solicitors, who testified that his client had been trying to evict her ex-husband from Heath House through all the legal channels open to her. As yet she had been unsuccessful but he was of the opinion that the courts would eventually secure Dale's removal, possibly within eighteen months. He confided to the court that he had received a great many letters from the Baroness over the years, some of which were couched in amusingly melodramatic terms. He concluded by saying that in his opinion she was a most remarkable woman.

Opening for the defence on Wednesday, 26 July, Anthony Arlidge told the court that the Baroness's children, Marcus and Sophia, would not be called, even though they were at Heath House on the day their father was murdered as the baroness did not wish them to suffer the trauma of giving evidence on her behalf. Once this had been clarified the moment came that everyone had been waiting for—the calling of the Baroness de Stempel to give evidence. She walked almost casually towards the witness box, carrying her spectacle case. There was absolute silence as everyone leaned forward, anxious to hear her take the oath in clipped but barely audible tones. The rows of journalists were unusually animated, heads down, scribbling furiously.

Questioned by Anthony Arlidge the Baroness answered firmly but so quietly that Mr Justice Owen, anxious that the jury should hear her answers clearly, allowed her to sit on his left, in a seat reserved for visiting dignitaries. Unfortunately, this didn't resolve the problem for there was no microphone. She was therefore asked to resume her stand in the witness box where she remained for the rest of the day. Although she told the court that her ex-husband had once struck her so hard at the base of her spine she was still in constant pain, she refused the Judge's invitation to sit whilst giving evidence—she did, however, accept a glass of water, from which she sipped from time to time.

She confirmed many of the points made in one of her statements to the police, parts of which had been read to the court by a police officer earlier in the proceedings. She had refused, she said, to participate in anal sex with her husband who considered her inhibited. 'He was very sexually active and aggressive, but it was certainly not loving,' she said. She had also told police that on one occasion she had seen Dale through a window at Heath

191

House 'wearing lipstick, tatty trousers and socks and a pair of ladies' high heeled shoes'. Lynne Williams, Dale's home help, had already testified that she had seen two pairs of ladies' shoes in his bedroom. She did not specify the size, however—Dale took size 12 shoes—and it is quite possible, of course, that they belonged to a house guest.

The Baroness also stated that as the marriage soured Simon Dale was often moody and sullen and was violent towards her and the children, in whom, she said, he showed 'little interest and no affection at all'.* He often smacked the boys but 'could never catch' Sophia. Once, when Susan found Simon chasing Marcus around the table in the kitchen, she flew to his defence by kicking her husband in the groin—on another occasion she threw a piece of coke at him, causing a nasty graze on his temple. Furthermore, she claimed, they had no social life whatever because, in her opinion, Dale was 'boring and mean'.

When the supremely confident Anthony Palmer, bristling with antagonism, rose to confront the Baroness the rise in tension was tangible. Without mincing his words he suggested that she was a cunning and clever woman and the reason she went back to Heath House the day after the murder was to return the cleaned up jemmy to its usual place on the back of the cottage door.

'You can suggest that until you are blue in the face—that is not true,' she retorted. And, confirming her solicitor's earlier testimony, she added: 'It doesn't make sense for me to have killed that man. The court was going to get him out cleanly and legally.'

The antipathy between them seemed genuine as Palmer continued with his examination and, during a particularly heated exchange, he suggested that she had killed Dale through her overwhelming sense of anger and frustration over his blatant refusal to leave Heath House.

To this, the Baroness answered: 'Bollocks, Mr Palmer! That's absolute nonsense.'

---

*According to Terry Kirby in his book *The Trials of the Baroness*, Alexander, Sebastian and Marcus retained a bond with their father despite the family rift and their memories of childhood are far from unhappy.

As the word left her lips the long row of journalists, wedged tightly along the benches in the press box, bent forward as one and started writing. One reporter, not quite believing his ears, looked across at another who nodded delightedly in affirmation. The court officials remained commendably impassive and the judge, after a barely discernible pause, continued to write in his notebook whilst Anthony Palmer demanded: 'I beg your pardon?'

'That is absolute nonsense,' said the Baroness, slightly adjusting her reply. She must have been exhausted when she left the witness box at the end of that day for she had withstood six hours of relentlessly aggressive questioning with remarkable fortitude.

The following day Anthony Palmer rose to deliver his closing speech for the prosecution. 'This was not,' he suggested, 'a planned and premeditated murder; this is a matter that started, as so many domestic matters do, with a build-up of events and then a sudden explosion.' Describing the Baroness as a 'witty, clever, very, very determined and spirited woman' he said that possession of Heath House had become a battle between two very stubborn and embittered parties both desperate to win. Finally, he invited the jury to bring in a verdict of manslaughter if they felt quite unable to agree on the murder charge.

When the court reassembled the next day Sebastian, Marcus and Sophia made their first appearance in the public gallery and listened attentively as Anthony Arlidge rose to deliver his closing speech in defence of their mother. He proclaimed, in his calm and measured manner, that the prosecution case rested entirely on circumstantial evidence. It was true, he said, that his client had been at Heath House on the day of the murder, but, he suggested, Simon Dale would never have opened the door to his ex-wife. As for the jemmy referred to in the case, it did not fit exactly with the wounds found on Simon Dale's body—'any firm, blunt, angular instrument could have done it,' he argued. Finally, he reminded the jury that the police 'for all their exhaustive inquiries' found not a single item of forensic evidence to link his client with the crime.

When the court resumed on Monday, 31 July, the heat from outside had already begun to pervade the sombre interior. Mr

Justice Owen, surrounded by piles of notebooks and court files, began the difficult task of summing up all the evidence for and against the prisoner. His voice was authoritative, but with a mellow, almost fruity quality, rather like that of the film actor, Trevor Howard. He summarised all the evidence with scrupulous attention to detail and told the jury to ignore the fact that the Baroness had used certain colourful expletives for, he mused, 'words which our grandfathers would not have used are today used in mixed company'.

But he did express some concern that the Baroness had revealed certain of Dale's sexual proclivities during the proceedings. At this, Anthony Arlidge rose swiftly to object, reminding the court that his client had only made statements to the police about her ex-husband's alleged penchant for cross-dressing and anal sex, as at the onset of the enquiry they had asked her specifically for any information that might have a bearing on the case. She had mentioned the incidents for that reason only, in that he may have had contacts, unknown to the police, with similar inclinations.

At one stage in his summing up the judge waggled the jemmy above his head and emphasised that it was the jury's grave duty to decide for themselves whether this was, as the prosecution alleged, the weapon used by the murderer—or was it, he asked, simply a tool in common use around the gardens of Heath House? He later urged the jurors to record a verdict of manslaughter if they honestly felt that the Baroness had been so provoked by her ex-husband's behaviour that any reasonable person would have lost control. Alternatively, he said, they must find her either guilty or not guilty of murder.

At eleven o'clock that day the jury retired to consider their verdict, leaving members of the public and journalists to gather in groups in the great hall where it was cool or on the sun scorched steps outside. Everyone was talking about the case—many of the journalists felt that Arlidge had the edge, whilst others felt that Palmer had presented an equally convincing case. Three of the Baroness's children—Sebastian, Marcus and Sophia—gathered in an anxious group with a few friends. The tension was clearly

Sophia and Marcus

showing on their faces, though Sophia, a pretty young woman
with many of her mother's mannerisms, managed a few fleeting,
nervous smiles. And somewhere in the cool belly of the huge
building, the Baroness waited.

No one strayed far in the heat of that afternoon for fear of
missing the finale of the drama that had enthralled them for so
long. When the court was eventually reassembled at 2.45 p.m.
there was a rush for seats. Twenty-eight journalists representing
nearly all the national newspapers hastily commandeered a few
inches on the press bench. Everyone looked towards the dock as
the Baroness ascended the steps and slowly resumed her seat. She
was flanked by two wardresses. The court rose as the judge
entered and took his seat. As the jurors filed in from the back of
the court one of them looked directly at the Baroness and smiled.

Minutes ticked by as the legal formalities were observed. The
Foreman of the jury affirmed that a verdict had been reached.
There was absolute silence in the court. As he said the words
'Not guilty', cheering broke out in the public gallery but,

controlled to the last, the Baroness simply smiled and calmly clasped her hands together. At this point a young man sitting in the public gallery with Marcus and Sophia leaned over the balustrade and dropped a small bunch of orchids at the Baroness's feet. She stooped to retrieve them, looked up and smiled briefly before descending the steps once more.

The verdict, however, did not make the Baroness a free woman. As she left the court, still carrying her flowers, she seemed genuinely pleased to see the hoard of press photographers and wellwishers waiting outside. Though remote and expressionless in court she smiled readily for the cameras and waved as she was driven away in a white taxi accompanied by a female police officer—not, however, to celebrate her acquittal or return to the cottage at Docklow, but back to prison to await yet another trial, on a charge of theft, fraud and forgery of Lady Illingworth's will. Charged with her were Marcus, Sophia and Baron Michael de Stempel.

The fraud trial, at the Queen Elizabeth II Crown Court in Birmingham, began on 19 February, 1990, and lasted for ten weeks, ending on 21 April. Marcus was sentenced to 18 months for his part in the fraud, Sophia 30 months and the Baron 4 years. Referred to by the judge, Mr Justice Curtis, as 'the mastermind' behind the whole conspiracy to defraud Lady Illingworth, the Baroness, who had pleaded guilty to all seven charges, received a sentence of 7 years. She was released on August 6, 1992, having served 5 years of her sentence.

On 19 May, 1990, a memorial service for Simon Dale was held at the little church of St Edward, near Hopton Castle. His son Sebastian, who gave an emotional address, was joined by his brother, Alexander, and a number of Dale's closest friends, who, fiercely loyal to the memory of Simon Dale, felt that he had somehow been forgotten in all the sensational publicity connected with the case.

In the autumn of 1991 the police searched Heath House and its grounds for gold bullion worth in excess of £10,000,000. It was alleged that 29 gold bars were once stored in a cellar of Lady

Illingworth's house in Grosvenor Square. They were last seen in 1967 and now appeared to be missing. After a five day search, involving six police officers using metal detectors, no gold was found.*

Undoubtedly the central figure in the whole extraordinary affair is the Baroness de Stempel, now known as Cecilia, not Susan, a woman who on the one hand displays iron self-control in public yet has always, it seems, become intensely involved with charismatic, flamboyant and, at least for her, unsuitable, men.

And even her dissenters and adversaries have admitted that, whatever her failings may be, she is extraordinary. On a television programme shortly after the conclusion of the Birmingham trial Chief Superintendent David Cole said this:

'She is an extremely intelligent and articulate person. She is also, no doubt, a very cunning person and she very cleverly manipulated affairs to her own ends. She is also quite a domineering person and she is able to, I think, manipulate those closest to her to become her lieutenants in the whole affair... She can be witty and charming and considerate and on the other hand there's another side to her—she can be patronising, dismissive, haughty and she can show an unpleasant side to her character—there's no doubt about that.'

Admitting that he, too, found her remarkable, Chief Inspector Mike Cowley of the Fraud Squad, nevertheless felt that she was also 'totally and utterly ruthless and very, very evil'. Yet, according to a man who had worked for her at Weobley, the Baroness was anything but evil. 'She was a nice woman to me,' he said. 'Perfectly friendly in a stiff sort of way. Good on the teas. You didn't lack for a cup of tea there. I liked her. All this wicked woman stuff—wasn't on as far as I'm concerned.'

Cecilia de Stempel is clearly a self-contained, reserved and unconventional woman with a passion for privacy, certainly not

---

* In May, 1990, writs were served on the Baroness and three of her children—and the Baron—on behalf of the Illingworth estate, asking for the return of 'chattels and property converted by the family, and exemplary and aggravated damages for wrongful interference.'

the sort to spend hours exchanging platitudes over cups of coffee but it is preposterous to suggest that this makes her, as some witnesses have maintained, a sinister recluse.

And finally, to return to the murder of Simon Dale. Surely a woman of the Baroness's intelligence, if she *had* killed her ex-husband, would have had the foresight to remain hidden that Friday evening and, moreover, to think up a more plausible alibi than spending the evening alone, watching, of all things, an Agatha Christie film on TV. And surely, had she known she would be questioned, she would have chosen some activity other than spending the weekend washing the clothes she was wearing on the day of the murder and polishing a poker that belonged to Heath House—an incredibly convenient piece of the jig-saw if, that is, the tragic killing of Simon Dale had been yet another work of detective fiction. And is it really conceivable that she would have left the cooker on and risked losing her precious Heath House, after all her efforts to re-possess it—by fire?

Furthermore, if she *had* murdered Dale she would have known that the police would arrive on her doorstep once the body was found. Why then, did she make no attempt to clear the cottage at Docklow of all Lady Illingworth's treasures which, on her own admission, she had acquired illegally? A few trips in a transit van would have saved her an awful lot of trouble. Clearly, she had no reason to imagine for one moment that the police were about to enter that Alladin's cave and had Simon Dale not been killed the fraud would have, in all probability, remained undetected, or at least, unpublicised.

Undoubtedly, there are some people who, despite her acquittal, remain convinced that the Baroness was guilty as charged and, when asked, will say that in their opinion she was extraordinarily lucky to 'get away with it'. Nothing will convince them of her innocence, until, that is, the murderer of Simon Dale is found. Unfortunately, it is possible that time could eventually so distort memory that the verdict at Worcester Crown Court will be conveniently forgotten and real life will become legend.

Bibliography

Davies, Dewi *Law and Disorder in Breconshire* D.G. & A.S. Evans

Gaute, Joe & Odell, Robin *Exhumation of a Murder* Harrap 1975

Gaute, Joe & Odell, Robin *Murder 'Whatdunit'. An Illustrated Account of the Methods of Murder* Harrap, 1982

Green, Jennifer *The Morning of Her Day* Divine Books, 1987

Hale, Leslie *Hanged in Error* Penguin Books, 1961

House, W.H. *Presteigne Past and Present*

Huggett, Frank E. *Life Below Stairs* Book Club Associates, 1977

Koestler, Arthur & Rolph, C.H. *Hanged by the Neck. An Exposure of Capital Punishment in England* Penguin Books, 1961

Kirby, Terry *The Trials of the Baroness* Mandarin, 1991

Lustgarten, Edgar *A Century of Murderers* Methuen 1975

Moore, Ann *Curiosities of Herefordshire* SB Publications, 1992

Nash, Jay Robert *World Encyclopaedia of 20th Century Murder* Headline, 1992

Palmer, Roy *The Folklore of Hereford & Worcester* Logaston Press, 1992

Pierrepoint, Albert *Executioner: Pierrepoint* Harrap 1974

Smith, Eldon *Crime & Punishment in England & Wales* Gomer, 1986

Wharton, Kate *Blood Money. The Story of the Baroness de Stempel* Ebury Press, 1991

Whitmore, Richard *Victorian & Edwardian Crime & Punishment* Batsford, 1978

Wilson, Colin & Pitman, Patricia *Encyclopaedia of Murder*

Young, Filson, ed. *The Trail of Herbert Rowse Armstrong* William Hodge, 1927

Also the following journals were consulted:

John Bull
The Brecon & Radnor Express
The Cambrian
The Carmarthen Journal
The Daily Telegraph
The Forrester
The Hereford Journal
The Hereford Times
The Lancet
The London Illustrated News
The Police News
The Shropshire Star
The Times
The Welshman

Index